Evaluating Instructional Leadership

For every school leader who bravely embraces the leadership challenge, for every family member and friend who unconditionally embraces our educational passion.

Evaluating Instructional Leadership

Recognized Practices for Success

Julie R. Smith
Raymond L. Smith
Foreword by John Hattie

CORWIN
A SAGE Company

FOR INFORMATION:

Corwin

A SAGE Company

2455 Teller Road

Thousand Oaks, California 91320

(800) 233-9936

www.corwin.com

SAGE Publications Ltd.

1 Oliver's Yard

55 City Road

London EC1Y 1SP

United Kingdom

SAGE Publications India Pvt. Ltd.

B 1/I 1 Mohan Cooperative Industrial Area

Mathura Road, New Delhi 110 044

India

SAGE Publications Asia-Pacific Pte. Ltd.

3 Church Street

#10-04 Samsung Hub

Singapore 049483

Printed in the United States of America

A catalog record of this book is available from the Library of Congress.

ISBN 978-1-4833-6672-2

Executive Editor: Arnis Burvikovs

Associate Editor: Desirée A. Bartlett

Editorial Assistant: Andrew Olson

Production Editor: Amy Schroller

Copy Editor: Allan Harper

Typesetter: C&M Digitals (P) Ltd.

Proofreader: Dennis W. Webb

Indexer: Jean Caselegno

Cover Designer: Leonardo March

Marketing Manager: Lisa Lysne

This book is printed on acid-free paper.

15 16 17 18 19 10 9 8 7 6 5 4 3 2 1

Contents

Foreword   vii

    John Hattie

Preface   xi

Acknowledgments   xvii

About the Authors   xix

Chapter 1: The Challenge   1

Chapter 2: The Architecture of Instructional Leadership Ability   21

Chapter 3: Element 1: Establishing a Shared Vision/Mission,
Goals, and Expectations   45

Chapter 4: Element 2: Strategic Resourcing   55

Chapter 5: Element 3: Ensuring Teacher and Staff Effectiveness   67

Chapter 6: Element 4: Leading and Participating in
Teacher/Leader Learning and Development   79

Chapter 7: Element 5: Providing an Orderly, Safe,
and Supportive Environment   91

Chapter 8: Feedback for Learning   103

Chapter 9: Deliberate Practice in Theory   123

Chapter 10: Deliberate Practice in Application   143

Chapter 11: Putting It All Together   151

Resources   163

Bibliography   167

Index   173

Foreword

John Hattie

Four years ago we decided to mount a new course for school principals. One of the requirements from the University was that we had to first hire a marketing company to survey prospective clients about what they would want in such a course. From close to 3,000 senior teachers and school leaders the marketing company found that they wanted six features in any course they would undertake: how to handle accountability, how to improve (particularly given changes in technology), how to cope with personal challenges such as "wearing a number of hats," how to be an administrator, and how to better use infrastructure in their school. When asked for the major reason they would engage in a university degree the conclusion was that they wanted "to gain a spectrum of skills, particularly team development and management skills, innovative approaches and the ability to communicate with staff students and parents." They were also asked for the specifics within courses, and the top 20 included topics such as leading a learning community, managing difficult people, leading self and others, managing personalities, assessment and development of staff, leading the management of the school, engaging and working with parents and the community, managing diversity in a school, and curriculum leadership and management. Hardly at all was there reference to enhancing the instructional impact, leading the debates about what "impact" meant in this school, or building a coalition of success in the school about learning.

Needless to say, we did not listen to the market and call the degree Master of School Leadership, or offer many of the courses and topics listed above. Yes, leaders need to be good administrators, yes they need to be good at people management, and yes they need to be good at ensuring an orderly flow and sense of fairness in the school — but these are baseline conditions and they are not the main game. The primary function of school leaders is none of these. It is instructional leadership — it is ensuring that there is a collective collaboration of all the adults in the school to have an agreed understanding of what impact means in this school (and certainly hope it is not just a narrow impact on test scores), agreed understanding of the sources of evidence about the magnitude of this impact, and an equity focus on ensuring all students share in this impact. An efficient administration and high levels of management is merely the base for doing this instructional work. The course is called Masters of Instructional Leadership and has a dominant component about how to have debates about impact, how to know what impact looks like and how it can be evaluated in the school, how to build a coalition of success around those who have maximized impact and then invite all others into this coalition, how to coach teachers to know their impact and plan lessons based on evidence of impact, and how to engage students in these processes.

This book — along with Jim Popham's *Evaluating America's Teachers: Mission Possible?*—could well be the text for this course. It not only highlights the key messages about the role of the leader, but it is does so in a way that is engaging and practical and reflects the Smiths' long history of being school leaders, teaching school leaders, and seeing the effects of their own teaching. I have seen the Smiths in action, separately and together, and they know how to lead and how to teach, they have a strength of purpose they do not waver from, and these attributes come through this book.

Their message is unequivocal — leadership is about managing the conditions of schools to impact on student learning. The book is about how to evaluate this impact. They are quite dismissive of many of the current leadership methods. If you were a man from Mars or lady from Venus, and read the principal-evaluation systems around the United States, you would think that principals spent all day ticking boxes, observing others to then tick boxes, and spending much time ensuring the right boxes were available to be ticked. It is hard to find research literature showing that observing teachers and completing the typical evaluations make much difference to much anything — except we get more reliable at ticking boxes. Does this type of activity affect student lives? Hardly. Certainly, many of the evaluations of teachers, particularly classroom observation, have low impact because the observations are of the teachers, not the impact of the teachers on students. Indeed, I argue (too strongly perhaps) that it is a sin to go into a class and watch a teacher teach — as all that happens is that we tell the teacher how they could have taught more like us. The primary purpose of classroom observation is to observe the impact of the teacher on the student (whoops, there go many of the current observations out the window).

The Smiths point to the research that shows that leaders who focus their attention on evaluating the impact of teachers on student learning are more likely to be successful at enhancing that impact. Such a leader focuses his or her attention on such practices "as relentlessly pursuing clear goals, aligning and allocating available resources to the pursuit of those goals, planning, coordinating, and evaluating both the teaching as well as the curriculum, encouraging and joining in teacher learning and development, and ensuring an orderly and supportive environment is likely to have more positive impacts on student achievement and well-being than other leadership practices."

But doing all this is not enough — as it can be done at various levels of excellence. Throughout the book there is focus on distinguishing between evaluative actions that do not meet expectations, progressing, proficient, and exemplary. This is progression we are all on, and every day we need to match our actions to these standards of excellence. This is why school leaders continually strive to enhance their performance. This is why we get new cohorts of students and often new teachers every year to challenge us to again be exemplary. This is the challenge of school leadership that is not as common in many other businesses.

One of the greatest powers of a school leader is that they have the power to create the narrative in their schools. Is it a narrative of curriculum, tests scores, bus timetables, tracking — the peripherals of schooling that need sorting; or is the narrative about the impact of all the adults in the school on student learning — learning in its widest sense? The Smiths suggest that that narrative should be about *knowing* the quality of the impact of the instructional programs in the school (and all else serves this narrative). Hence they place much reliance on the presence of excellent evaluation of these programs.

Their evaluation plan is quite focused. It follows a "backward design" approach that has been found to be successful in many parts of the teaching and learning process. That is, it asks leaders to start at the end; what are the impacts you want to achieve, what it would look like in this school when the school is "successful," what are the skills that we would expect principals to know and be able to do, and what sources of evidence would be demonstrating that we have this impact? This can be an iterative process (including learning at the end for the next round of evaluation). But these questions precede the management, the deciding about resources, the choice of evaluation methods, the collection of evidence, and the weighting of these sources of evidence.

Our experience in our Masters course mentioned above is that there is an additional core skill — the proficiency to interpret the evidence we collect. Too often, evaluation is seen as collecting data, and indeed schools are awash with data. But the skill is interpretation; that is, making sense of the evidence to then make consequential decisions and actions. This is among the hardest skills to learn, and often it requires multiple interpretations, triangulating the first set of interpretations, sharing and seeking critique of the interpretations — and this takes much character as well as skill. You may be wrong!

This character strength is based on inner convictions, and they outline the major mind frames that school leaders need to develop: the conviction or mind frame to start with the question, "My role as leader in this school is to evaluate my impact," to then deliberately activate change, to relentlessly focus on learning and the impact of teaching, to see assessment as feedback to me as teacher and leader, and to engage in dialogue. To do this, the leader needs to embrace the challenge, build relational trust, advocate the vocabulary of learning, and never shy from the hard work that is leading learning.

I commend the chapters about how to achieve these lofty goals. Indeed the first set of skills relate to establishing shared goals across the school. To do this, the exemplary leader has to have good management and person-management, hence chapters on strategic resourcing, how to lead, and how to create an orderly, safe and supportive environment. These are the bases of excellent evaluations of impact. And all this does not happen in a haphazard or random manner — it needs to be deliberate. This skill of deliberately charting the voyage is a fundamental skill of leaders. The Smiths provide many case studies to exemplify how to be deliberate.

Perhaps the most attractive aspect of this book is that it emphasizes that evaluation is for a purpose and not an end itself. The aim of evaluation is to discover the worth, merit, or significance of the programs that we implement in our schools. The aim is to learn and empower those who deliver the programs to adapt, replace, or continue. It is about identifying where exemplary practice is occurring, and often such success is all around us — if only we knew. And that is the point of this book.

—*Professor John Hattie*
Director, Melbourne Education Research Institute
Melbourne Graduate School of Education
University of Melbourne

Preface

The more leaders focus their influence, their learning, and their relationships with teachers on the core business of teaching and learning, the greater their influence on student outcomes. (Robinson, Hohepa, & Lloyd, 2009, p. 40)

In his book *Assessing Educational Leaders,* Doug Reeves (2009) convincingly argues that "leadership evaluation systems [are] the 'perfect storm' of failure" (p. 1), with the confluence of many different variables at the same time creating a particularly destructive series of consequences. The first variable is a growing national shortage of educational leaders, which is joined by the second force, "A leadership evaluation system that simultaneously discourages effective leaders, fails to sanction ineffective leaders, and rarely considers as its purpose the improvement of leadership performance" (Reeves, 2009, pp. 2–3).

Specifically, Reeves supports this highly critical view of principal-evaluation systems by suggesting that three issues plague effective principal-evaluation systems. First, many of these evaluation systems contain poorly defined, ambiguous standards replete with educational jargon that tends to be substituted for clearly expressed language. The second problem involves undefined standards of performance. That is, even if the evaluation system has removed confusing educational jargon and ambiguity from its standards, it fails to adequately distinguish performance that is making progress but is not yet proficient from performance that is exemplary. Third, at times, these documents hold principals responsible for the actions of others without the authority to compel those actions in others.

The first two forces are joined with a third commanding force, the expectations of local, state, and federal authorities, that requires a rather dramatic change in the role as well as the performance of education leaders, extending well beyond prior definitions of administrative responsibilities. Clearly, the responsibilities of education leaders now exceed what individual leaders in schools and school districts can be expected to carry out alone (Reeves, 2009).

Specifically, here is what a state education agency (SEA) and its local educational agency (LEA) must do with their principal-evaluation programs in order to successfully obtain flexibility approval from the Elementary and Secondary Recovery and Reinvestment Act Flexibility Program. To receive this flexibility, an SEA and each LEA are required to

Develop, adopt, pilot, and implement, with the involvement of teachers and principals, teacher and principal evaluation and support systems that: (1) will be used for continual improvement of instruction; (2) meaningfully differentiate performance using at least three performance levels; (3) use multiple valid measures in determining performance levels, including as a significant factor data on student growth for all students (including English Learners and students with disabilities), and other measures of professional practice (which may be gathered through multiple formats and sources, such as observations based on rigorous teacher performance standards, teacher portfolios, and student and parent surveys); (4) evaluate teachers and principals on a regular basis; (5) provide clear, timely, and useful feedback, including feedback that identifies needs and guides professional development; and (6) will be used to inform personnel decisions. (U.S. Department of Education, 2012, p. 3)

In brief, while high-quality management within a school is necessary—where children are happy and well behaved, the school is orderly, the facility and property are well cared for, and the finances are under control—it is not a sufficient condition for leadership effectiveness. Why? Because it requires, in addition, that the school's management procedures ensure high-quality teaching and learning for all (both students and staff). If effective leadership is about improving instruction and making a bigger difference to adult and student learning, then the SEA and LEA need trustworthy advice about the types of leadership as well as the specific sets of leadership practices that are most likely to deliver on those outcomes—the primary basis for summative evaluation.

The good news is that, while the last half-decade has produced a wealth of thinking in the area of leadership but a scarcity of research in leadership evaluation, we still have—thanks to the efforts of a few educational scholars (which we will explore shortly)—improved clarity about the practices of highly effective principals and the components to effective leadership evaluation systems. The bad news is that states across the nation appear to be compelled to follow the same path with principal evaluation as the one that they have pursued with teacher evaluation by constructing summative leadership evaluation documents that have far too many performance indicators to effectively keep track of or measure accurately when evaluating principals. What is needed is a principal-evaluation procedure that focuses solely "on [those] aspects of leadership that are most critical for student learning" (Seashore-Louis, Leithwood, Wahlstrom, & Anderson, 2010, p. 215) and let go of the rest.

For example, the Minnesota State Model for principal evaluation consists of five performance measures in which 31 indicators are nested, the Colorado State Model Evaluation System for Principals and Assistant Principals is made up of six quality standards supported by 25 elements, the Washington State Principal Evaluation Model is made up of eight criteria buoyed by 28 elements, the Massachusetts Model System for Educator Evaluation comprises four standards and 20 indicators that are sustained by 42 elements, and the Florida Model School Leaders Assessment entails 45 indicators that support 10 standards of practice within four domains, to name a few.

In brief, while all of these models of principal evaluation imply a desire to formatively develop principals, in many cases the formative, improvement-oriented virtues of these evaluation systems may, due to the number of leadership practices being assessed, diminish the practicality of providing principals the formative as well as the summative, evaluation-focused dividends of the strategy. As a result, these "fat" documents lead some within our field feeling as if current evaluation systems are too time-consuming, contain too many items, and include too many redundant concepts to effectively evaluate the impact of leadership on student learning.

A NEW VISION OF PRINCIPAL EVALUATION

Whether it is the celebrated Italian artist Michelangelo sculpting the statue of David, or the famous American architect Frank Lloyd Wright designing The Guggenheim Museum, the renowned Russian-American novelist, philosopher, playwright Ayn Rand penning *Atlas Shrugged,* or, in our case, two educational authors and researchers devising a way to effectively assess school leaders' instructional leadership ability, all successful endeavors begin with a vision. In other words, just as the sculptor envisioned the beautiful figure of David trapped within the block of marble and the novelist scrawled John Galt to life on blank pages of her manuscript, each needed a clear vision of what he or she hoped to accomplish and so too did we as we visualized what an instructional leadership assessment system could and should look like. In reality, "all things are created twice" (Covey, 1989, p. 99). For all things, there is a mental (first) construction and a physical (second) construction. The physical follows the mental, just as the school's collective improvement efforts follows the school's school improvement plan development.

Although many authors have addressed the topic of vision development, perhaps the most insightful efforts in this area come from the writing of Jim Collins and Jerry Porras in *Built to Last.* Drawing upon a six-year research project at the Stanford University Graduate School of Business, Jim Collins and Jerry Porras (1994) studied several high-profile exceptional and long-lasting companies (e.g., 3M, Wal-Mart, Walt Disney, Boeing, Sony, and Hewlett-Packard) to answer the question, "What makes the truly exceptional companies different from their competitors?" Throughout their research, the authors kept "looking for underlying, timeless, fundamental principles and patterns that might apply across eras" (p. 17). In the process, they discovered that one of those *timeless, fundamental principles* was the interminable value of a good vision. Vision, they state, "defines what we stand for and why we exist . . . and sets forth what we aspire to become, to achieve, to create" (p. 221).

With these thoughts in mind, our vision for an effective process for growing and assessing school leaders' instructional leadership ability can best be presented using the format of a resolution. In general a *resolution* in the context of debate by an assembly is a formulation of a determination, expression of opinion, etc., submitted to an assembly or meeting for consideration. That is, a proposal is put to a meeting, the proposal is debated, and a resolution is adopted. In a similar manner, we are proposing to you, the reader, the need for a new principal-evaluation framework, which we intend to discuss over the course of this book in hopes that, by the time you finish the book, you will be compelled to adopt our new vision as your own. What follows, then, is a series of arguments for a new vision in the form of *whereas statements* that culminate in a *therefore statement,* or our vision. In brief, by "employing a point-by-point whereas-based analysis" (Popham, 2013, p. 34), we intend to establish a clear rationale for the basis of this book. At the conclusion of our analysis, a description will be provided regarding what an instructional leadership ability evaluation should look like—our vision, which is described in the remaining chapters.

- *Whereas* most principal-evaluation instruments measure far too many domains of leadership practice that outstrip both the time and energy of evaluators, thus they lack depth and focus on those leadership practices that research has shown to be significantly related to the impact on student and teacher performance, and
- *Whereas* many principal-evaluation systems fail to focus on the critical behaviors principals perform to influence student achievement, and
- *Whereas* many principal-evaluation systems currently in use consist of ambiguous standards or the performance expectations are unclear, rather than operating on clear definitions of performance levels and precise rubrics that allow evaluators to effectively measure aspects of leadership performance, and
- *Whereas* an axiom of good evaluation as well as a lesson in common sense suggest that multiple, not single, sources of evidence be utilized when evaluating a principal, and
- *Whereas* significant variations exist in not only in the quality of principal-evaluation evidence, but also in its relative importance

when appraising a specific principal, the evaluative weight of all principal-evaluation evidence sources must be judged individually and then tailored to the particular principal's school level, context, and to the principal's level of experience; and

- *Whereas* principal growth plans tend to be utilized as a way to mitigate less-than-proficient leadership performance, rather than be used as a continuous improvement tool with all principals from the most novice to the most veteran within the school system,

- *Therefore*, principal-evaluation systems should be based on weighted-evidence judgment in which principal evaluators initially select, richly describe, and weight a parsimonious number of leader-quality criteria that focus on the most important behaviors and actions that improve instruction and student learning, use multiple sources of evidence, craft growth plans for all principals that address individual learning needs, determine whether to adjust those weights because of a leader's distinctive school level, context, and level of experience, and, last, arrive at a coalesced judgment regarding a leader's quality.

As a result of this analysis, its six supporting arguments are (1) principal-evaluation instruments distract attention away from those leadership practices that are closely linked to increases in student achievement and teacher performance, (2) they tend not to focus on the leadership practices that matter the most, (3) they are populated with vague and unclear performance expectations that do not allow evaluators to effectively measure leadership performance, (4) they should require that more than one source of evidence be used to evaluate a principal, (5) the evaluative weight of multiple evidence sources first must be determined separately and second must be individualized to the particular principal's school level, context, and level of experience, and (6) growth plans are natural byproducts of principal-evaluation systems and are useful tools for continuous improvement for all principals, regardless of their prior level of leadership performance.

Evaluating *Instructional Leadership: Recognized Practices for Success* is designed both as a summative evaluation of leadership performance and as a growth model to improve leadership performance, thereby increasing the likelihood that teacher and student performance will also improve. We have taken the position that district leaders can and in most cases must simultaneously fulfill two roles: that of a formative coach as well as that of as summative evaluator of school principals. With all due respect to our friend and colleague Dr. Jim Popham (2013), who argued that anyone who believes "that a combined formative and summative [evaluation effort] can succeed are most likely to have recently arrived from outer space" (p. 18), we came to the position that district leaders must serve two masters (formative coach as well as summative evaluator) not because we believe that these are the ideal roles but because we see this as being the most practical arrangement. That is, we rarely see school districts that have the staffing luxury to hire both a central office administrator whose sole function it is to be a coach or mentor of school leaders and their professional growth and at the same time hire another district administrator who only facilitates the summative evaluation process for school leaders.

The book acknowledges the forces described earlier that have created this "perfect storm" in school leader-evaluation systems and describes a practical approach that school and central office leaders can take to create and successfully implement an evaluation of instructional leadership framework that will have a significant impact on leadership, teacher, and student performance. Moreover, the book utilizes the research that identifies the type of leadership practices that are most directly related to increases in student achievement and its related elements (Robinson, Lloyd, & Rowe, 2008), with the principal and assistant principal of the school as the focal points. As we shall show, the book describes a process that will encourage schools and districts to

- move beyond an event that occurs once every year, long after any opportunity to influence leadership performance;
- provide frequent feedback for school leaders with multiple opportunities for continuous improvement;
- focus on remarkably specific, high-impact, research-based aspects of leadership performance in order to significantly increase student achievement;
- describe in specific terms the difference between performance that is exemplary and performance that is proficient, progressing, or not meeting leadership expectations thereby establishing clear, coherent, and fair expectations for present and future leaders;
- be used to improve the performance of a 20-year veteran as well as to coach the most novice assistant principal; and
- also be used to train new leaders and to identify and hire prospective leaders.

The audience for this book is threefold: First and foremost, this book is for principals and all school leaders who want to make a greater impact than they ever imagined they could; second, it is for central office leaders who are in a position to alter the educational system, thereby creating conditions for transforming the principalship into a powerful force for reform; and third, would-be aspiring leaders, teachers who are seeking opportunities to expand their impact beyond the classroom and move into entry-level school leader positions.

Acknowledgments

Writing a book is certainly a journey in personal growth. It has become very clear to us that writing is less about declaring what you know and more about being ready to accept learning coming your way. Over the past thirty-four-plus years, our leadership beliefs and practices have been shaped, challenged, and refined by some of the most influential educational thinkers in the world. We have had the great pleasure and privilege to learn from leaders such as Michael Fullan, John Hattie, Viviane Robinson, James Popham, Doug Reeves, Bob Marzano, Rick Dufour, Jim Knight, Larry Ainsworth, Brian McNulty, Art Costa, James Kouses, Barry Posner, Tom Peters, Stephen Covey, Larry Lezotte, Jim Collins, Donald Schön, Everrit Rogers, Tom Guskey, Warren Bennis, Chris Argyris, Roland Barth, Peter Senge, Thomas Sergiovanni, William Daggett, Liz Wiseman, Malcolm Gladwell, John Maxwell, and Todd Whitaker, who have all reinforced our belief that our ability to grow as a leader is based on our ability to grow as a person. The opportunity to coauthor this book with each other and to engage in spirited conversations to ensure that we upheld the integrity of our research and leadership beliefs has certainly caused us to grow as leaders and learners both professionally and personally. We are forever grateful for your lasting influence.

One of Professor Hattie's mindframes is *learning is hard work*. Authors also know that writing is hard work. When it seemed impossible to find the time to write this book, we had our Corwin cheerleaders encouraging us to write just a little every day and to continually remind us that this was the right work. We would like to acknowledge the unconditional support of Kristin Anderson, Arnis Burvikovs, and Ariel Price. School and district leaders also know that leading is hard work, and the hard work of Sherry Bees, Tucker Harris, James Neihof, Keith Peters, Ted Toomer, and Rob Zook is showcased in our book; these individuals serve as role models for their peers and are powerful examples of instructional leadership in action.

Most importantly, it was our commitment to all of the school and district leaders we have had the opportunity and great fortune to work with over the years—there are far too many to mention—and to all the teachers and assistant principals who will move into new school/district leadership positions in the next decade that ultimately inspired this book.

PUBLISHER'S ACKNOWLEDGMENTS

Corwin gratefully acknowledges the contributions of the following reviewers:

Kathy J Grover
Superintendent, Clever R-V Public Schools
Clever, MO

Lyne N. Ssebikindu
Assistant Principal, Crump Elementary School
Memphis, TN

Kelley King
Educational Consultant, Author
Head of Lower School, San Diego Jewish Academy
San Diego, CA

Marsha Carr
Superintendent
Wilmington, NC

Peter Dillon
Superintendent
Great Barrington, MA

About the Authors

Dr. Julie R. Smith is a thirty-four-year veteran educator, speaker, consultant, and author. She currently serves as an Author Consultant with Corwin Press. Her passion, area of focus, and expertise is in building leadership capacity within people and systems; school improvement planning; and teacher, principal, and district evaluation models. Julie served as an adjunct professor at the University of Colorado Denver Health Sciences Center and taught at Florida Atlantic University in their aspiring leader programs. She also was an Executive Director of Elementary Schools in Cherry Creek School District in Colorado.

Julie continued to pursue her focus and passion in leadership development by coauthoring a book on principal evaluation entitled *The Reflective Leader: Implementing a Multidimensional Leadership Performance System* (2012). In addition to writing about leadership and leadership development, Dr. Smith continues with her learning by providing seminars in North America and Canada around leadership development and Professor John Hattie's research in Visible Learning as a Visible Learning[Plus] Consultant with Corwin. She is also trained to provide workshops in Dr. James Popham's research around designing and implementing defensible evaluations programs and Dr. Russ Quaglia's research involving student aspirations and student voice.

Dr. Raymond Smith is an Author Consultant with Corwin Press. Prior to joining Corwin, Dr. Smith served as adjunct professor at the University of Colorado Denver Health Sciences Center, teaching within a principal-preparation program; Dr. Smith currently works with Florida Atlantic University in their aspiring leader program. Dr. Smith's diverse experience includes over 38 years of teaching and leadership at the building (high school principal), central office (Director of Secondary Education), and university levels.

Subsequent to completing his doctorate in educational leadership and innovation in 2007, Dr. Smith pursued his area of specialty and passion in leadership development by authoring several articles for the Ohio Department of Education, coauthoring two books: *School Improvement for the Net Generation* (2010) and *The Reflective Leader: Implementing a Multidimensional Leadership Performance System* (2012).

In addition to writing about leadership and leadership development, Dr. Smith is an activator of learning, leading others in workshops around Professor John Hattie's research in Visible Learning as he is one of 21 Visible Learning[Plus] Consultants with Corwin. He also conducts workshops in Dr. James Popham's research around designing and implementing defensible teacher evaluation programs, and Dr. Russ Quaglia's research involving student aspirations and student voice.

The Challenge

I nasmuch as the research on principal leadership in general has developed into a growing body of thick scholarship, the research on principal-evaluation systems remains surprisingly thin. This is concerning given the fact that nearly 60% of a school's total impact on student achievement is attributable to effective teacher and principal practices (Seashore-Louis et al., 2010), with the impact of leadership alone being described by some as the single most important factor in moving schools forward (Fullan, 2010a). In brief, while highly effective leaders are essential to school reform efforts and the exercise of effective leadership practices has been shown to have a strong, measurable effect on student achievement, teaching quality, and schools, our current evaluation practices treat these key players as nonessential employees. So, what can we learn from the research that is available on principal-evaluation systems?

PRINCIPAL-EVALUATION RESEARCH

To begin with, several recent surveys and reviews of principal-evaluation systems and instruments have yielded important lessons from the field. For example, Douglas Reeves (2009) surveyed more than 500 leaders from 21 states and reviewed more than 300 evaluation instruments in order to assess both the qualities of the leadership evaluation instruments as well as the experience of leaders being evaluated within the context of their work. Reeves concluded, among other things, that standards were vaguely worded, that feedback was tardy at best and absent at worst, and that the evaluation process itself is unhelpful to the improvement of leadership practices.

Ellen Goldring and her associates (2008) analyzed 65 evaluation instruments in order to take a deep look at what and how districts evaluate principals. These authors found that there was little congruency in performance areas, format, and levels of specificity among the analyzed evaluation instruments. Furthermore, they discovered that the leadership qualities that matter the most (i.e., rigorous curriculum and quality instruction) were given the least coverage within the evaluation instruments. The authors concluded that, more often than not, the assessment of leadership practices was missing justification and documentation related to the utility, psychometric properties, and accuracy of the instruments.

Next, operating on the belief that principal voices should be present within the national, state, and local dialogue about the redesign of principal-evaluation instruments, Matthew Clifford and Steven Ross (2010) convened elementary, middle, and high school principals to outline a framework for principal evaluation. Based on their review of the research on principal evaluation, they recommended that principal evaluations include compound measures of student, school, and principal achievement and take into account the context of school environments.

Last, Davis , Kearney, Sanders, Thomas, & Leon (2011) conducted one of the more comprehensive reviews of the literature to determine what research reveals about principal-evaluation systems. The authors identified a number of important conclusions about the status and descriptions of principal-evaluation systems before moving to recommendations for and best practices in the design of more effective principal-evaluation systems. Although Davis et al. identified a dozen recommendations for more effective evaluations, three of those 12 stood out as they reflect similar conclusions to those that Matthew Clifford and Steven Ross found in their work: (1) evaluations should reflect multiple evidence-gathering methods, (2) evaluation systems should accommodate variations in school contexts and environments, and (3) the most effective principal evaluations are those that are focused on a few high-impact actions.

In addition to these findings, the research that we reviewed regarding the effects of principal evaluation revealed that, in general

- Principal-evaluation systems lack depth and also lack focus on the right things (Goldring et al., 2008; Seashore-Louis et al., 2010; Mitgang, Gill, & Cummins, 2013).
- Principals perceive performance evaluation as having limited usefulness in the areas of feedback, professional learning, and accountability to school improvement (Portin, Feldman, & Knapp, 2006).
- Principal-evaluation systems contain vague performance expectations and/or lack clear norms or performance standards (Goldring et al., 2008; Reeves, 2009).
- Principal-evaluation systems have not been implemented in ways that promote accurate judgments of principal effectiveness (Clifford & Ross, 2011; Davis et al., 2011).

- Principal-evaluation systems are typically one-size-fits-all systems that do not differentiate for different school contexts (Clifford & Ross, 2011; Davis et al., 2011; Mitgang et al., 2013).
- Principal-evaluation systems have not been tested for critical psychometric properties and are not based on the latest research on principal leadership practices (Clifford, Menon, Gangi, Condon, & Hornung, 2012; Davis et al., 2011).
- Many principal-evaluation systems, not unlike many other educational initiatives, are poorly implemented (Kimball, Milanowski, & McKinney, 2009).

Consequently, a major challenge is for principal leadership evaluation to be used effectively as a benchmark for personnel functions, as a means to leverage within school leaders' day-to-day performance those leadership practices that are most directly related to increases in student achievement, as a powerful communication tool for providing and securing both summative as well as formative feedback from and to a school leader, and as a means of setting organizational goals for school leaders' professional development. Clearly, our current principal-evaluation practices must change in order to maximize the impact of school leaders on learning and student achievement. It is time for a better and more focused principal-evaluation system!

POSITIVE EFFORTS THAT ARE RESHAPING THE PRINCIPAL-EVALUATION LANDSCAPE

Despite the generally dreadful state of principal evaluation, there have been several significant efforts in the right direction. The Interstate School Leaders Licensure Consortium (ISLLC), for instance, has performed an extensive comprehensive and research-based review of principal and school effectiveness and has clearly articulated many of the practices in which leaders need to be engaged in order to succeed in the 21st century. Moreover, subsequent to the development of the ISLLC Standards in 1996, more than 40 states have adopted them in their entirety or as a template to guide policy-making or the development of their own specific leadership performance expectations. Thus, the ISLLC Standards have significantly reshaped the principal-evaluation landscape by focusing states and local education associations on principals' behaviors and actions.

In addition to the ISLLC Standards, two recent studies have clearly revealed the leadership qualities that are essential for improved student achievement and have dramatically changed the role of the principal. For example, Viviane Robinson and her colleagues (Robinson, Lloyd, & Rowe, 2008) have helped to shape the leadership evaluation landscape by clearly defining the type of leadership as well as the specific practices that have shown to have the most significant impact on student learning.

What they discovered was that a leader who focuses his or her attention on such practices as relentlessly pursuing clear goals; aligning and allocating available resources in the pursuit of those goals; planning, coordinating, and evaluating both the teaching as well as the curriculum; encouraging and joining in teacher learning and development; and ensuring an orderly and supportive learning environment is "likely to have more positive impacts on student achievement and well-being" (p. 668) than those who focus on other leadership practices (i.e., inspirational motivation, individualized support, accessibility, etc.), which tend to positively influence teacher attitudes but rarely have an impact on student outcomes. Therefore, district office leaders who are responsible for principal evaluation, along with principals themselves, must make certain that they plan for and ensure that frequent high-impact instructional leadership practices routinely occur within the school community in order to have the most significant impact on student learning and well-being (see the Resources section for a crosswalk of the ISLLC Standards to our framework).

Karen Seashore-Louis et al. (2010) join with Robinson et al. (2008) in helping educators understand the leadership practices that matter the most to teachers and therefore to students and their learning! This investigation helps shape principal-evaluation systems and is particularly noteworthy because of the size of its database (with inclusion of data from nine states, 43 school districts, and 180 schools), the use of multiple theoretical and methodological approaches to their research (with inclusion of both qualitative and quantitative data), and the comprehensive sources of leadership examined (with inclusion of data from the state, district, school, classroom, and community levels). The authors' six-year study attempted to describe successful educational leadership and to explain how such leadership can foster changes in professional practice, yielding improvements in student learning. Numerous findings and implications for policy and practice were reported; the most important finding, however, was that "leadership practices targeted directly at teachers' instruction (i.e., instructional leadership) have significant, although indirect, effects on student achievement" (p. 10).

The ISLLC Standards, Viviane Robinson's descriptions of leadership practices that matter the most, and Karen Seashore-Louis and colleagues' efforts to clarify the leadership actions that seem to lead to improved student learning all represent significant steps forward in our efforts to reform and improve principal-evaluation systems. Consequently, the findings of research on the current state of principal evaluation; the contributions from the ISLLC; the efforts of researchers such as Karen Seashore-Louis, Kenneth Leithwood, John Hattie, Viviane Robinson, and countless others; and our own practical experience as principals and central office leaders have reshaped our concepts of what an effective principal-evaluation framework looks like. What follows is a step-by-step description of how we created a single-criterion leadership evaluation framework.

CREATING A SINGLE-CRITERION PRINCIPAL-EVALUATION FRAMEWORK

In the late summer of 2013, Corwin asked us to join a cadre of leaders selected from across the United States and the Canadian provinces to take part in a three-day Corwin Teacher-Evaluation Academy structured around the contents of a 2013 Corwin book entitled *Evaluating America's Teachers: Mission Possible?*, by Dr. W. James Popham. The Academy was taught by the author himself, a lively, passionate, learned, and witty gentleman, and his objective was to build capacity within a group of professional development consultants to be able to work with state departments and ministries of education, school districts, and school principals to help them avoid four serious mistakes found in the implementation of most teacher evaluation systems—mistakes that, if made, "can cripple a teacher-evaluation system" (p. 12). The three-day training session was very insightful. You probably are asking yourself why we are talking about teacher evaluation in a principal-evaluation book.

The reason we are talking about teacher evaluation is that the same five-step process that Dr. Popham utilizes in his book to develop a "weighted-evidence judgmental evaluation of teachers" (Popham, 2013, p. 36) reflects the steps that we went through to determine our leadership evaluation framework, with one small variation. We added a sixth step to Dr. Popham's work. These six steps include (1) choosing the evaluative criterion, (2) creating rubrics that describe what principals should be expected to know and be able to do within each criterion, (3) identifying the evidence source(s) to represent each evaluative criterion, (4) designating an evaluative weight to each evidence source selected, (5) determining whether any evaluative weights should be adjusted based on principal experience or school context, and (6) blending the multiple evidence sources into an overall judgment about a particular principal's quality. A depiction of the six steps is presented in Figure 1.1, followed by a description of each step.

Step 1: Choosing the Evaluative Criterion

There is a reason why the first step is the first step. Clearly, the single most important decision to be made as we attempt to construct an instrument to evaluate principals is the evaluative criteria for determining a principal's quality and their impact on adult and student learning and achievement. In reviewing the many different examples of principal evaluation currently in use, it is immediately obvious that districts focus on a mixture of performance areas when evaluating principals, with an assortment of designs at various levels of distinction (Goldring et al., 2008). The variety of leadership performance evaluations that districts use, however, generally have their origin in one of four national leadership standards bearers: (1) ISLLC Standards, (2) National Board Standards for Accomplished

Figure 1.1   Six Steps in Establishing a Single-Criterion Evaluation Framework

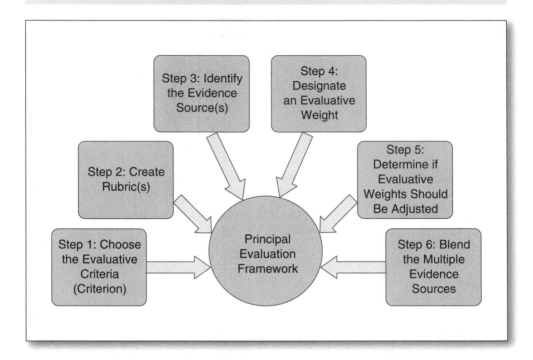

Principals, (3) the Vanderbilt Assessment of Leadership in Education's Core Competencies and Key Processes (VAL-ED), or (4) leadership standards or frameworks developed by the Mid-continent Regional Educational Laboratory (McREL) (Canole & Young, 2013). The performance expectations contained within ISLLC and National Board Standards are shown in Figure 1.2, and the performance expectations for VAL-ED and McREL are shown in Figure 1.3.

Once we retrieved these four sets of leadership performance expectations, we followed an inductive line of reasoning to detect patterns and regularities among the four sets of data to establish a rough draft synthesis of leadership expectations that we think is compact yet comprehensive. That is, we recorded each expectation verbatim onto a spreadsheet, read each repeatedly, grouped them together, merged items that were similar, and, based on a detailed analysis of the meaning of the items included, we developed a newly synthesized list. This rough draft synthesis is depicted in Figure 1.4.

Next, as we noted previously, given the fact that the authors of a number of current research studies on effective principal-evaluation systems argued for educational practitioners to narrow and deepen their focus on a few high-impact leadership practices (Goldring et al., 2008; Seashore-Louis et al., 2010; Davis et al., 2011) we filtered these seven leadership expectations

Figure 1.2   A Comparison of ISLLC and National Board Standards

ISLLC Standards	National Board Standards
• Setting a widely shared vision for learning • Developing a school culture and instructional program conducive to student learning and staff professional growth • Ensuring effective management of the organization, operation, and resources for a safe, efficient, and effective learning environment • Collaborating with faculty and community members, responding to diverse community interests and needs, and mobilizing community resources • Acting with integrity, fairness, and in an ethical manner • Understanding, responding to, and influencing the larger political, social, economic, legal, and cultural context	• Lead with a sense of urgency and achieve the highest results for all students and adults • Lead and inspire the learning community to develop, articulate, and commit to a shared and compelling vision of the highest level of student achievement and adult instructional practice . . . and advance the mission through collaborate processes that focus and drive the organization toward that vision • Ensure that teaching and learning are the primary foci of the organization • Ensure that each student and each adult in the learning community is known and valued . . . develop systems so that individuals are supported socially, emotionally, and intellectually in development, learning, and achievement • Inspire and nurture a culture of high expectations, wherein actions support the common values and beliefs of the organization • Skillfully lead the design, development, and implementation of strategic management systems and processes that actualize the vision and mission • Consistently demonstrate a high degree of personal and professional ethics exemplified by justice, integrity, and equity • Effectively advocate internally and externally to advance the organization's vision and mission • Encourage leaders to act as humble lead learners who make their practice public and view their own learning as a foundational part of school leadership

through the research results reported by Robinson et al. (2008) to determine which aligned with the leadership practices that had been determined to have the greatest impact on student achievement. Why pay attention to this research in particular you ask? Plainly put, their research is highlighted in John Hattie's (2009) international best-selling educational book entitled

Figure 1.3   A Comparison of VAL-ED and McREL Performance Expectations

VAL-ED	McREL

• Core Components
 	
  1. High standards for student learning—The extent to which leadership ensures there are individual, team, and school goals for rigorous student academic and social learning
 	
  2. Rigorous curriculum—Ambitious academic content provided to all students in core academic subjects
 	
  3. Quality instruction—Effective instructional practices that maximize student academic and social learning
 	
  4. Culture of learning and professional behavior—Leadership ensures that there are integrated communities of professional practice in the service of student academic and social learning
 	
  5. Connections to external communities—Leading a school with high expectations and academic achievement for all students requires robust connections to the external community
 	
  6. Performance accountability—There is individual and collective responsibility among the leadership, faculty, students, and the community for achieving the rigorous student academic and social learning goals
 	
• Key Processes
 	
  7. Planning—Leaders articulate a shared direction and coherent policies, practices, and procedures
 	
  8. Implementing—Leaders put into practice the activities necessary to realize high standards for student performance
 	
  9. Supporting—Leaders create enabling conditions; they secure and use the financial, political, technological, and human resources necessary to promote academic and social learning
	• Culture—Fosters shared beliefs and a sense of community and cooperation
	• Order—Establishes a set of standard operating procedures and routines
	• Discipline—Protects teachers from issues and influences that would detract from their teaching time or focus
	• Resources—Provides teachers with materials and professional development necessary for the successful execution of their jobs
	• Involvement in curriculum, instruction, and assessment—Is directly involved in the design and implementation of curriculum, instruction, and assessment practices
	• Focus—Establishes clear goals and keeps those goals in the forefront of the school's attention
	• Knowledge of curriculum, instruction, and assessment—Is knowledgeable about current curriculum, instruction, and assessment practices
	• Visibility—Has quality contact and interactions with teachers and students
	• Contingent rewards—Recognizes and rewards individual accomplishments
	• Communication—Establishes strong lines of communication with teachers and among students
	• Outreach—Is an advocate and spokesperson for the school to all stakeholders
	• Input—Involves teachers in the design and implementation of important decisions and policies
	• Affirmation—Recognizes and celebrates school accomplishments and acknowledges failures

VAL-ED	McREL
10. Advocating—Leaders promote the diverse needs of students within and beyond the school 11. Communicating—Leaders develop, utilize, and maintain systems of exchange among members of the school and with its external communities 12. Monitoring—Leaders systematically collect and analyze data to make judgments that guide decisions and actions for continuous improvement	• Relationship—Demonstrates an awareness of the personal aspects of teachers and staff • Change agent—Is willing to challenge, and actively challenges, the status quo • Optimize—Inspires and leads new and challenging innovations • Ideals/beliefs—Communicates and operates from strong ideals and beliefs about schooling • Monitors/evaluates—Monitors the effectiveness of school practices and their impact on student learning • Flexibility—Adapts his or her leadership behavior to the needs of the current situation and is comfortable with dissent • Situational awareness—Is aware of the details and undercurrents in the running of the school and uses this information to address current and potential problems • Intellectual stimulation—Ensures faculty and staff are aware of the most current theories and practices and makes the discussion of these a regular aspect of the school's culture

Figure 1.4   Rough Draft Synthesis of Leadership Expectations

Synthesis of Leadership Expectations
1. Establishing a shared vision, goals, and expectations
2. Developing, utilizing, and maintaining effective systems of communication among members of the school and with its external communities
3. Strategic resourcing
4. Ensuring teacher and staff effectiveness
5. Leading and participating in teacher/leader learning and development
6. Providing an orderly, safe, and supportive environment
7. Acting with integrity, fairness, and in an ethical manner

Visible Learning: A Synthesis of Over 800 Meta-Analyses Relating to Achievement. Additionally, the findings reported by Robinson et al. (2008) were cited in many of the research studies that we reviewed for this book. In short, their research is highly respected within the field. The results of this winnowing process (i.e., removing less important items from a larger list of items) can be seen in Figure 1.5, where we list the five elements of enhanced leadership practice. We chose the word *element* over other alternatives (i.e., *domains, standards,* etc.) as we believed that this word underscores the fact that each

Figure 1.5   Five Elements of Enhanced Leadership Practice

Elements of Enhanced Leadership Practice *Instructional Leadership Ability*	
Element	**Description**
Establishing a shared vision/mission, goals, and expectations	Involves the establishment, communication, and monitoring of performance as well as learning goals and expectations and the engagement of internal and external stakeholders in the process to achieve clarity and consensus in the vision and goals
Strategic resourcing	Involves linking the section and allocation of resources (i.e., money, people, and time) to the school's priority goals. Includes the recruitment, selection, and retention of staff with suitable expertise
Ensuring teacher and staff effectiveness	Includes the leader's direct involvement in supporting and evaluating teaching through frequent classroom observations, with feedback provided to and collected from teachers. Involves establishing a coherent instructional program, ongoing dialogue with teachers about the relationship between teaching and student achievement, and monitoring of student performance data to drive continuous program improvement
Leading and participating in teacher/leader learning and development	Involves leaders who both lead and participate with teachers in targeted professional development that is either formal or informal in nature
Providing an orderly, safe, and supportive environment	Involves creating an environment that provides assurances that teachers and students can focus on learning by setting and enforcing clear expectations, protecting teachers from outside pressures, and addressing staff conflict quickly and effectively

element is a fundamental, necessary part of the whole evaluation system and sufficiently conveys the scope and importance of a leader's work.

We settled on these five elements of leadership practices—practices that are associated with instructional leadership (Robinson et al., 2008)—because current research has concluded that the "mean effect size estimates for the impact of instructional leadership on student outcomes is three to four times greater than that of transformational leadership" (Robinson et al., 2008, p. 655). Specifically, the mean effect size (ES) for the impact of instructional leadership on student outcomes was 0.42, whereas the mean effect size for the impact of transformational leadership on student outcomes was 0.11 (Robinson, 2011). Effect size is a simple measure for quantifying the difference between two groups or the same group over time on a common scale. For example, an effect size of 0.40 indicates that the mean of the treated group is at the 66th percentile of the untreated group. That is, the average person in the treated group would score higher than 66% of the untreated group that was initially equivalent. As a general guide, an effect size of between 0.00 and 0.20 can be interpreted as showing no or weak effect; between 0.20 and 0.40, a small but possibly educationally significant effect; between 0.40 and 0.60, a moderate educationally significant effect; and greater than 0.60, a large and educationally significant effect.

Transformational leadership practices typically include such things as providing inspirational motivation, individualized support, direction, instructional support, monitoring of school activity, buffering staff from external demands, and accessibility. Although these transformational leadership practices are important, research suggests that they are not sufficient. In particular, Robinson et al. (2008) found that, while the transformational leadership practices had an impact on teacher attitudes, the effects generally failed to have an impact on student outcomes.

Moreover, as you can see when you compare Figure 1.5 with Figure 1.4, the list of leadership practices has been reduced from seven to five practices. We eliminated two practices: (1) developing, utilizing, and maintaining effective systems of communication among members of the school and with its external communities and (2) acting with integrity, fairness, and in an ethical manner. On the surface, the omission of these two leadership practices may cause the reader some concern. So let us explain the reasoning behind that decision.

Clearly, effective leaders must establish strong communication links between internal and external members of the school community. After all, communication is without question an important leadership capability. However, we would argue that, in addition to being able to communicate effectively, effective leaders also must rely on a number of other important leadership practices (i.e., a clearly articulated set of theories of action that underpins their every action in school and guides them to apply leadership content knowledge to resolve problems while at the same time building relational trust with students, staff, parents, and non-parent community members), which we discuss in greater detail in Chapter 2. In this sense, a leader's instructional leadership practices are like the branches of a living tree. These branches grow naturally out of a common trunk (representing their mission or a set of core beliefs or "mindsets" [Dweck, 2006] that guide their actions) and common roots (representing the theories of practice that give sustenance and life to their leadership practices). The relationship among theories of practice, mission, and leadership actions is depicted in Figure 1.6.

So, we decided to eliminate communication as a leadership practice because we agree with Viviane Robinson and her colleagues, who argued that this capability could be excluded as an instructional leadership practice because it is deeply embedded in all of the leadership elements (Robinson et al., 2008). In other words, effective leadership involves not only the task of decision-making but also the facilitation of staff discussions and the nurturing of trusting relationships that lead to shared solutions and good decision-making. In short, if leaders do not get the relationships right, it will be problematic for them to accomplish the task.

Figure 1.6   Relationship of Leadership Actions, Mission, and Theories of Practice

The second leadership practice that we eliminated was ethics. Inasmuch as we would strongly argue that high ethical standards for principals are necessary, we agree with the position taken by New Leaders for New Schools (2010), who stated that "this [matter] is best identified as a non-negotiable condition of employment" (p. 20) instead of as a stand-alone element with a range of performance levels. Therefore, we have removed these two items from the list and end Step 1 with five instructional leadership ability elements. More importantly, by winnowing down to five instructional leadership ability elements, we believe that we have effectively addressed the research finding that principal-evaluation systems typically lack depth and also lack focus on the right things (Goldring et al., 2008; Seashore-Louis et al., 2010). A focus on these five dimensions of instructional leadership ability, representing elements of a single criterion, is a focus on the right things.

Step 2: Creating Rubrics for Each Dimension

You will recall from our earlier comments that a second criticism of principal-evaluation systems was that many systems contain vague performance expectations and/or lack clear norms or performance standards (Goldring et al., 2008; Reeves, 2009). Step 2 calls for us to address this issue. Consequently, we have developed five rubrics (see Chapter 3 for details), one for each of the five instructional leadership elements, that make up the single criterion for instructional leadership ability. That is, we provide rich narrative descriptions (rubrics) of the instructional leadership performance elements themselves along with clear "word picture descriptions" (Hall & Hord, 2011, p. 48) of each dimension to deepen and enrich the reader's understanding of what each is expecting the school leader to know and be able to do—the expectations of instructional leadership ability.

Toward that end, the next five chapters, each one dedicated to a thorough development of a single instructional leadership ability element, is organized into four parts: A Rationale and Description of the particular element, the Evidence of Impact for that element, a chapter Summary, and a Rubric for the element. That is, for each element, a rubric has been created, made up of rich descriptions of leadership practice that are situated along a continuum ranging from exemplary practice on one end to not meeting standards of practice on the other. Additionally, these descriptions of practice are further subdivided into the components of the element or its critical attributes, and several possible authentic examples of what the instructional leadership ability practice looks like according to the degree of proficiency being practiced in order to invite self-assessment and formative feedback. There are four levels of performance: exemplary, proficient, progressing, and not meeting expectations (see Chapter 2 for a general explanation of each performance level). The rubric template can be seen in Figure 1.7.

Figure 1.7   Element Rubric Template

Name of Element			
	Exemplary	**Proficient**	**Progressing**	**Not Meeting Expectations**
Rubric Language	Descriptions of leadership practice			
Critical Attributes	Essential elements of the element			
Real-World Examples	Authentic examples of what the practice looks like			

Step 3: Identifying the Evidence Source(s)

Several groups of researchers have argued that principal evaluations should reflect multiple evidence-gathering methods (Davis et al., 2011; Clifford & Ross, 2011; Sanders, Kearney, & Vince, 2012) in order to capture the scope and complexity of new expectations. Consequently, this section describes the process that we went through to identify the evidence sources that would appropriately represent the established evaluative criteria. Identifying sources of evidence is important work in that the evaluative criteria themselves become consequential only when leader evaluators denote how a leader's performance status with respect to a given evaluative criterion will be determined.

A number of authors and researchers helped to shape our thinking as we worked our way through this step. For example, a joint Principal Evaluation Committee of practicing principals (i.e., representatives of elementary, middle, and high school principals who are members of the National Association of Elementary School Principals and the National Association of Secondary School Principals) convened in 2010 to outline a framework for principal evaluation (Clifford & Ross, 2010). The committee's suggested evaluations included multiple measures of student, school, and principal success that place value on the context of the school environment. Clifford and Ross identified six key domains within their ideal principal-evaluation system and identified measurement examples as a part of each domain. For instance, within the fifth domain, entitled

Professional Qualities and Instructional Leadership, they list the following measurement examples:

- "Portfolio artifacts of principal performance aligned to state, district or national professional standards;
- The degree to which a principal achieved goals from the previous year's professional growth plan;
- Observations of principal practice;
- Providing actionable feedback to teachers to improve practice;
- 360-degree surveys of faculty, staff and evaluators; and
- Self-reflections from principals" (p. 20)

Next, the Vanderbilt Assessment of Leadership in Education (VAL-ED) principal-evaluation system includes "an evidence-based, multi-rater rating scale that assesses principals' learning-centered leadership behaviors known to directly influence teachers' performance, and in turn students' learning" (Porter et al., 2008, p. 5). The VAL-ED survey instrument asks each respondent to consider the item describing a principal's behavior and, ahead of rating the principal on his or her effectiveness on that item, directs the respondent to identify what sources of evidence he or she used to make the rating. The sources of evidence that respondents can select include:

- Reports from others
- Personal observations
- School documents
- School projects or activities
- Other sources
- No evidence

The third system is the New Leaders for New Schools (2010) principal-evaluation system. Like the prior two evaluation systems, this system also promotes the use of multiple sources of evidence by principal managers in their assessment of principals. While the authors of this evaluation system support the use of multiple sources of evidence, they "do not offer a particular bundle of sources of evidence" (p. 24); rather, they recommend "some promising and useful options" (p. 24) for educational practitioners, such as

- Direct observation of leadership practice
- Surveys of parent perceptions
- Surveys of teacher perceptions
- School quality reviews
- Student performance data (especially in nontested grades)

Perhaps the most helpful document that we reviewed was the report from WestEd (Sanders et al., 2012), entitled *Using Multiple Forms of Data in*

Principal Evaluations: An Overview with Examples. Essentially, the authors provide an explanation about the use of multiple forms of data relative to principal-evaluation systems. The authors also present hypothetical examples as to how to use multiple forms of data that give states, districts, and organizations a range of options to consider when designing their own principal-evaluation system. Last, they provide a review of several leadership evaluation examples from the field (i.e., Arizona Framework for Measuring Educator Effectiveness, Colorado Principal Evaluation Framework, Florida Personnel Evaluation System, Maryland Educator Evaluation System, New Leaders Principal Evaluation System, New York City Principal Performance Review, Tennessee Teacher and Principal Evaluation Policy, and Washington D.C. Public Schools Effectiveness Assessment System for School-Based Personnel: IMPACT) and how they incorporated multiple forms of data within their respective principal-evaluation systems.

Based on our review of the aforementioned documents as well as our practical experience, we decided to operationalize the elements of instructional leadership ability by relying on five specific sources of evidence, namely, (1) *student learning* as reflected by changes in the scores of a school's students on the current end-of-year statewide accountability tests and the scores of those students on previously administered versions of these tests and teacher-made assessments; (2) *teacher effectiveness* as reflected in the percentage of teachers for whom a principal is responsible who make "effective" gains in student achievement results and the percentage of teachers who are evaluated as effective; (3) *teacher, student, and parent ratings* of a principal's instructional leadership ability as collected three times a year via brief, anonymously completed rating forms; (4) *professional growth* as measured by the degree to which a principal achieved goals from the current year's *Deliberate Practice* plan; and, (5) *leadership assessment* as measured by a supervisor's qualitative rating and observations.

Step 4: Designating an Evaluative Weight

The fourth major task in developing the instructional leadership ability framework calls for the weighting of each evidence source selected. In other words, for all the evidence sources that we have selected to represent the instructional leadership ability criterion, we must make judgments regarding how much evaluative weight we should give to each of those sources toward an overall evaluation judgment. For instance, the New York City framework stipulates that student achievement accounts for 32% of the total, principal goals for 31%, teacher effectiveness for 22%, and district goals 15%. The District of Columbia Public Schools requires that 50% of the total come from student achievement and 50% come from the six Leadership Framework Standards (i.e., 25% from the instruction standard and 15% each for the talent, school culture, operations, family and community, and personal leadership standards). The Colorado principal-evaluation model specifies that 50% of the principal-evaluation be based on the six professional Quality Standards: strategic leadership, instructional leadership, school cultural and equity leadership, human resource leadership, managerial leadership, and external development leadership. The other half of a principal's evaluation is based on the seventh Quality Standard, which measures the academic growth of students in their school.

Based on our observations from research and our own practice, we designed our principal-evaluation system with the following suggested evaluative weights (see Figure 1.8):

- 35% on direct measures of student learning as reflected in changes in the scores of a school's students on the current end-of-year statewide accountability assessment and those students' scores on previously administered versions of these tests in addition to classroom-based assessments;
- 15% on teacher effectiveness in improving student achievement;
- 10% on the percentage of teachers evaluated as effective;
- 5% on teacher, student, and parent ratings of the leader's performance;
- 15% on the leader's professional growth (Deliberate Practice); and
- 20% on instructional leadership ability assessment

This distribution of evaluative weights accomplishes a number of important goals. First, it makes improving student achievement, measured directly and as a result of teachers, 60% of the total evaluation (35% from direct measures of student achievement and 25% from teacher effectiveness). Second, it underscores the important function of school leaders to recruit, retain, and support effective teachers. Third, it values the importance of feedback from others' perspectives, which are intended to illuminate our judgments about a leader's instructional leadership ability because leaders' actions are not always perceived in the same manner in which they were intended. Fourth, it places appropriate emphasis on the continuous efforts of leaders to improve their practices against the critical elements of leadership practices. Last, it serves to focus school leaders' work on the right stuff, specifically, instructional leadership—those practices that have been proven to have the greatest impact on student performance.

Step 5: Determining if Evaluative Weights Should Be Adjusted

Step 5 calls for a personalized judgment about whether evaluative weights should be adjusted to take into account such context-related issues as community environments, school environments that are in need of transformation (i.e., low expectations for students and toxic adult attitudes), level of principal expertise (i.e., novice versus veteran), school level (i.e., elementary,

Figure 1.8   Evaluative Weight

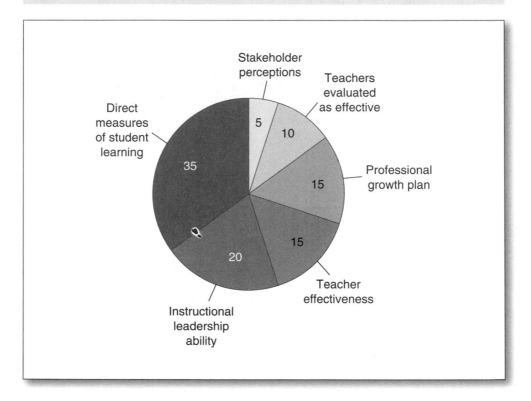

middle, high school), size of school, and school setting (urban versus rural). In an effort to provide direction to school districts as to how they can foster improvements in teaching and learning, Karen Seashore-Louis et al. (2010) observed that policies may need to be individualized to order to recognize "the importance of different school contexts, whether they are a result of demographic characteristics, administrator experience, school size, or school level. One-size-fits all policies will not" (p. 215) build confidence in the staff to meet very local needs.

A number of studies that we reviewed support the idea that district policies, including principal-evaluation policies, need to flex relative to individual school contexts (Davis et al., 2011; Portin et al., 2006; Clifford & Ross, 2010). Most notable, however, were the recommendations from New Leaders for New Schools (2010), which supported the research findings in a fairly straightforward manner. Specifically, they identified three specific ways in which school systems might suitably adjust expectations and still hold performance expectations at a high level: (1) differentiate for level of leadership expertise (i.e., novice versus veteran) so that principal managers can place more weight on "the accomplishment of leadership expectations and less on student achievement results" (p. 25), (2) differentiate for the school level in an effort to address the inherent differences between the jobs of a secondary school principal and an elementary school principal, and (3) differentiate evaluative weights based on the school's position on the improvement continuum, that is, whether the school is just beginning to establish school practices to counter toxic cultures and ineffective adult actions or whether the school has highly refined adult practices that adequately support all levels of student achievement. We believe that the three simple, candid, research-based approaches that New Leaders for New Schools suggest as a way to differentiate evaluative weights make practical sense, and therefore we have applied them to our framework.

Step 6: Blending the Multiple Evidence Sources

The final task in this six-step process required us to pull all of the pieces together so that a final, overall evaluation of a leader can be made. Inasmuch as this blending of evaluative evidence can be played out on a variety of levels of complexity, we suggest employing a very straightforward approach, as reflected in Figure 1.9. You will notice that this approach consists of a number of different features. First, each of the five measures is arranged in a tabular format. The evaluative weights for all five evidence measures are presented in the form of percentages in parentheses, immediately to the right of the label for each measure. For example, Measures of Student Learning has an evaluative weight of 35%. Second, you will also see that three of the five measures (Measures 1, 2, and 5) include multiple evidence sources, whereas the other two (Measures 3 and 4) use a single evidence source. In total, then, we are employing eight evidence sources. Third, the far right column reflects the number of points out of 100 potential points that could be earned by the leader for each evidence source. Last, at the very bottom of Figure 1.9, you will see that we have provided a qualitative scale for determining overall instructional leadership ability.

SUMMARY

In this chapter, we reviewed some of the key research to date on principal evaluation. Although this research has been found to be lacking in quantity, the quality of the conclusions being made within this research is sufficient enough to suggest that improvements are long overdue. However, several bright spots in this rather dismal picture were highlighted. Clearly, the continuing efforts of organizations such as The Council of Chief State School Officers, National Board for Professional Teaching, Vanderbilt University, the National Associations of Elementary and Secondary School Principals as well as researchers such as Matthew Clifford, Steven Ross, Ellen Goldring, Joseph Murphy, Karen Seashore-Louis, Kenneth Leithwood, and Viviane Robinson to provide leadership in this area are helping to positively reshape the leadership evaluation landscape. These organizations

Figure 1.9 Summative Evaluation

Instructional Leadership Ability Summative Evaluation		
Name: **School:**	**Date:**	
1. Measures of Student Learning (Evaluative Weight = 35%)		
Growth in State Assessments	out of	25
Classroom-Based Assessments	out of	10
Subtotal	**out of**	**35**
2. Measures of Teacher Effectiveness (Evaluative Weight = 25%)		
Improving Student Achievement (percent ≥0.40 ES)	out of	15
Teachers Evaluated as Effective	out of	10
Subtotal	**out of**	**25**
3. Measures of Others' Ratings of Leader's Performance (Evaluative Weight = 5%)		
Teacher, Student, and Parent Survey Ratings	out of	5
Subtotal	**out of**	**5**
4. Measures of Leader's Professional Growth (Evaluative Weight = 15%)		
Deliberate Practice	out of	15
Subtotal	**out of**	**15**
5. Measures of Instructional Leadership Ability Assessment (Evaluative Weight = 20%)		
Instructional Leadership Ability Assessment	out of	15
Observation		5
Subtotal	**out of**	**20**
GRAND TOTAL =	**out of**	**100**
District-Designated Overall Instructional Leadership Ability Categories: Exemplary = 91 or more out of 100, Proficient = 75 to 90, Progressing = 64 to 74, Not Meeting Expectations = Less than 64		

and authors helped to crystallize our views on principal evaluation, which we presented in a six-step process. Each of the six steps that we went through were discussed, and decisions leading up to the establishment of a single-criterion leadership evaluation system were revealed.

The Architecture of Instructional Leadership Ability

You will recall from our discussion in the last chapter that an effective leader must routinely engage in a number of important instructional leadership elements that give sustenance and life to their leadership practices in order to confidently engage in those practices. Consequently, our series of five instructional leadership ability elements clearly reflects critical leadership practices, but they are silent on the underlying leadership skills, capabilities, and theories of practice that are vital to the successful implementation of those leadership elements. So, why, you might be asking yourself, have we elected not to include those critical leadership skills in our evaluation model? The best answer is, we have taken the position that effective implementation of these five instructional leadership elements occurs because leaders are faithfully employing a common set of leadership capabilities or theories of practice as to how one thinks about his or her role as leader (Hattie, 2012a).

For instance, in ensuring teacher effectiveness, effective leadership practice most certainly involves frequent classroom observations of teachers' impact from instructional practice, followed by specific feedback to the teacher (i.e., Leadership Element 3). More important, however, is to make certain that the feedback that leaders provide to teachers helps them learn about their influences on students and thus gives them vital just-in-time information so they can change, enhance, or continue their teaching methods (i.e., Theory of Practice 1, "Evaluating Your Impact"). Thus, what is needed is the careful integration of leadership theories of practice that support specific instructional leadership practices. Hence, we believe that these foundational theories of practice reinforce the five structural elements and sustain the single evaluation criterion of instructional leadership ability, as depicted in Figure 2.1.

We intentionally selected a depiction of a Roman temple to represent the architecture of our evaluation framework for several reasons. First, just as the Roman architects designed and the builders constructed these magnificent edifices with the idea that they were "meant to last," we too have taken the same approach with our evaluation framework. Second, they erected their buildings on solid foundations to support the weight of the structure just as our evaluation model is built on a robust groundwork of research to sustain essential leadership practices. Next, the platform is designed to bear the weight of the columns. In our instance, our platform consists of nine theories of practice supporting the five Doric columns of leadership practice, with one column for each of the five instructional leadership ability elements: (1) shared vision and expectations, (2) strategic resourcing, (3) teacher and staff effectiveness, (4) teacher and leader development, and (5) an orderly and safe environment. In brief, the nine theories of practice sustain

Figure 2.1   The Architecture of Instructional Leadership Ability

the five elements and come together to form the instructional leadership ability framework. The remainder of this chapter briefly describes the nine theories of practice, the five elements of instructional leadership ability (depicted in Figure 2.1), and the four levels of leadership performance.

NINE THEORIES OF PRACTICE

Inasmuch as the research on the capabilities that are required for effective instructional leadership should inform the development as well as the evaluation of instructional leaders (Fullan, Hill, & Crevola, 2006), that research is surprisingly thin. The good news, however, is that several researchers have developed some important insights into these critical leadership capabilities. For example, Stanford University psychologist Carol Dweck (2006), in decades of research on achievement and success, has described two "mindsets," each of which "profoundly affects the way you lead your life. It can determine whether you become the person you want to be and whether you accomplish the things you value" (p. 6). That is, if you believe that your qualities or capabilities are established from birth and are immutable, then you hold a "fixed mindset" (p. 6). If, on the other hand, you believe that your innate qualities or capabilities are enriched over the course of your life as a result of your effort and perseverance, then you have a "growth mindset" (p. 7).

Additionally, Robinson (2010) recently performed one of the best syntheses to date of published empirical research evidence that illuminates the capabilities required to engage in effective instructional leadership. In her synthesis, she identified four research studies that she believed held the greatest promise for yielding insights into the capabilities required for effective instructional leadership (Nelson & Sassi, 2000; Leithwood & Steinbach, 1995; Bryk & Schneider, 2002). Her analysis resulted in the identification of three critical leadership capabilities: (1) utilizing relevant knowledge, (2) solving complex problems, and (3) building relational trust.

Last, John Hattie (2012a) in his book entitled *Visible Learning for Teachers: Maximizing Impact on Learning* posits that, in order for leaders (and teachers) to have a powerful impact in schools and classrooms, we have to change the way they think about their roles. Toward that end, he identifies eight "mindframes" (p. 159) that he believes must "underpin our every action and decision in a school" (p. 159) in order to have a major impact on student learning. Professor Hattie has subsequently added a ninth mindframe. The nine mindframes include "a belief that we are evaluators, change agents, adaptive learning experts, seekers of feedback about our impact, engaged in dialogue and challenge, and developers of trust with all, and that we see opportunity and error, and are keen to spread the message about the power, fun, and impact that we have on learning" (p. 159).

Whereas these three authors have identified critical leadership capabilities as a result of their research, it is important to note that Robinson, Hohepa, & Lloyd (2009) had earlier observed, in their *Best Evidence Iteration Report* for the Australian Ministry of Education regarding the particular leadership practices that are crucial for improving student outcomes, that "it is likely that additional [capabilities] may also be important for school leadership" (p. 174) to incorporate within their routine practice. We concur and have subsequently merged Carol Dweck's (2006) thinking on "mindsets" and Viviane Robinson's three capabilities with John Hattie's (2012a) nine "mindframes," which we have enhanced by adding additional leadership perspectives and identified nine common *theories of practice*, which buttress our five instructional leadership ability elements and together form the architecture of our instructional leadership ability framework.

ENGAGING IN COMMON THEORIES OF PRACTICE

Getting teachers and leaders to adopt these theories of practice is no easy task. However, changing the hearts and minds of teachers and leaders is an essential lever to making and sustaining long-term change (Fullan, 1998). Consequently, leaders and teachers alike must understand that behavioral changes almost always precede changes in their beliefs (Fullan et al., 2006). So, what are these powerful behaviors and ways of thinking that are "likely to have major impacts on student learning?" (Hattie, 2012a, p. 160). The nine Theories of Practice (TOP), which are briefly described in Figure R.4 in the Resources section of the book, represent individual and organizational beliefs requiring changes in how leaders' view their roles and practices. The Theories begin with a belief that leaders are those who evaluate their impact; activate change; focus on learning over teaching; use assessment as feedback; engage in dialogue; embrace the challenges of teaching, learning, and leadership; develop relational trust; teach the academic vocabulary of learning; and reinforce that learning and leading is hard work. A brief description of these leader behaviors follows.

TOP 1: Evaluating Your Impact

Leaders believe that their most essential undertaking is to continuously evaluate their impact on staff and students and, based on the results, alter, enhance, or continue their leadership strategies. In a formative sense, enacting this theory requires teachers to alter their instruction "on the fly" (Hattie, 2012a, p. 160) on the basis of student feedback about the effect of instructional practices used. It also means, however, that principals must make the same "just-in-time" adjustments to their leadership practice on the basis of the formative evaluation from teachers as to the impact of the leadership strategies that they have employed. It may seem odd to say that leaders need to become more expert at evaluation. After all, teacher evaluation is a major function of all principals' roles. However, in this context, evaluation means that principals need to enhance their evaluation skills about the effects that they are having on teachers. In this sense of the word, effective principals acting on this belief would, for example, be routinely collecting evidence on such things as teachers' perspectives on the effectiveness of the feedback that they are providing teachers as a result of routine classroom observations and making the necessary adjustments in their practice to increase their impact on teachers. It might also mean that principals are routinely conducting focus groups to better understand the degree of effectiveness of staffing decisions so that they can improve the decision-making process used to establish the school's master schedule.

From a summative point of view, operationalizing this theory of practice would mean that leaders are systematically evaluating the impact that they and their teachers are having on student learning by calculating, analyzing, and using effect size data from such measures as schoolwide reading, writing, mathematics progress; teacher-by-teacher comparisons as well as student-by-student comparisons; and comparisons of the top 20% of students with the bottom 20% of students in reading, writing, mathematics to name a few. Moreover, these effect size calculations should be made on an ongoing basis and display a disposition of the leader to constantly question what needs to be improved and/or taken to scale and what evidence is needed to support next steps. Toward that end, leaders need to know which influences (i.e., school, teacher, and leadership) make the greatest difference to student outcomes and prioritize these influences at the same time that they modify and/or eliminate those that do not make a difference. Critical questions that leaders might be attempting to answer in this particular theory of practice are reflected in Figure 2.2.

TOP 2: Activating Change

Leaders operate under the notion that success and failure in student learning is a byproduct of their action or inaction. That is, they see themselves as drivers of cognitive change, which requires a belief that student and/or adult achievement is not a fixed trait but rather a dynamic, constantly changing characteristic as a result of leader perseverance, dedication, and hard work (Dweck, 2006). It is about leaders having confidence in their ability to cause learning to happen for all teachers and students regardless of the teachers' prior experience or the students' poverty level and other uncontrollable demographic influences. It is also about leaders being willing to challenge the status quo and understanding the benefits of providing clear learning intentions and success criteria related to the school's most critical improvement targets. Leaders who are activating change and helping teachers see that achievement is changeable and "enhanceable,"

Figure 2.2   Critical Questions for Evaluating Your Impact

✓ What evidence might I gather that would convince me that this influence is working?

✓ In what ways might I compare this influence with that influence?

✓ What is the degree of significance of the effect on student learning?

✓ What evidence would I accept that I mistakenly used these methods and resources?

✓ Where is the evidence that shows that this program or practice is superior to other programs and other practices?

✓ Where has this practice been implemented such that it yields effective results that would convince my teachers and me to adopt it on the basis of the magnitude of the effects on learning?

✓ How does my conception of progress compare with other leaders' within the district?

✓ How do my leadership practices compare with those that the research suggests are most impactful?

for instance, would make certain that teachers are individually and collectively monitoring, measuring, and analyzing the relationship between their practice and the impact on student results. Thus, leaders understand that the degree to which students and teachers and leaders learn or not is based primarily on what they do or not do. Critical questions that leaders might be attempting to answer in this particular theory of practice are depicted in Figure 2.3.

TOP 3: Focusing on Learning More Than Teaching

Highly effective leaders thrive on discussions about learning rather than on discussions about best practices in teaching and leadership. That is, they see themselves as "Michelangelos" of learning, where the ongoing dialogue attempts to illuminate how both students as well as adults learn, to secure evidence of learning that occurs in multiple ways, and to understand how to acquire multiple learning strategies to fit a particular need and/or situation. Learning is hard work and is not always an enjoyable exercise (Hattie & Yates, 2014); consequently, leaders must first recognize that while Hattie's (2009) *Visible Learning* research applies to adolescents between the ages of 4 and 20 years, the theories of practice apply to adult learning as well (National Research Council, 2000). This point is particularly important because incorporating the theories of practice into educational practice will require a good deal of adult learning. In brief, the theories of practice and

Figure 2.3   Critical Questions for Activating Change

✓ How are we challenging all students regardless of family socioeconomic status other uncontrollable demographic influences?

✓ In what ways are we encouraging help-seeking behaviors within staff as well as within students?

✓ How are we helping students and staff acquire and use multiple learning strategies?

✓ How effective have we been at developing assessment-capable students and teachers?

✓ Have we identified and are we reinforcing the use of student and teacher learner qualities?

✓ How are we encouraging peer (teacher-to-teacher, teacher-to-principal, principal-to-teacher, student-to-student) interactions in order to improve learning?

✓ In what ways are we developing teacher self-regulation skills and growing the notion of teachers as students of their own effects to improve learning?

their implications for discussing learning and designing learning environments apply equally to the child as well as to the adult.

Second, because learning places a good deal of stress on mental resources, making it a difficult and slow process that is in many cases an uncomfortable experience, leaders must follow a recipe in order to cook up an effective batch of learning for teachers that focuses on (1) time, (2) goal-orientation, (3) supportive feedback, (4) accumulated successful practice, and (5) frequent review (Hattie, 2009). Consequently, principals demonstrating the belief that learning is the focus of their work would make certain, for example, that their professional development focus is on a small number of new learning opportunities with clearly articulated learning intentions and success criteria, that allow teachers to do them well (i.e., with time, monitoring, feedback, follow-up support, and just-in-time teaching), within the context of their work, and in concert with other key initiatives (Fullan, 2010b). During routine classroom observations, these same principals would be looking at the impact of teaching practices on student learning and offering feedback rather than focusing only on what the teacher is doing irrespective of its effect on students. Critical questions that leaders might be asking themselves in this particular theory of practice are reflected in Figure 2.4.

TOP 4: Viewing Assessment as Feedback About Impact

Leaders take the point of view that assessment is feedback to them regarding their leadership impact. Consequently, leaders, just like teachers with

Figure 2.4   Critical Questions for Focusing on Learning More Than Teaching

✓ Are our learning goals clearly articulated, few in number, and measurable?

✓ Have we as staff co-created our success criteria that result from our professional learning?

✓ What are teachers and leaders learning from their self-assessments against the success criteria and what next steps are we taking toward our learning intentions?

✓ Where and when in our day-to-day interactions do we as a staff have collegial debates about learning and about our impact on this learning?

✓ Are my classroom observations focused on teachers' strategies or on the impact those strategies are having on student learning?

students, need to identify and use "rapid formative assessment" (Yeh, 2006), that is, short-cycle formative assessment opportunities conducted frequently that provide invaluable information about their effects on teachers. Leaders, much like their students, need to have a clear understanding of the learning intentions that they are pursuing, where their performance is in relation to those goals, and what next steps might look like toward goal attainment. Critical questions that leaders should be asking themselves are shown in Figure 2.5.

Figure 2.5   Critical Questions for Viewing Assessment as Feedback About Impact

✓ Whom, which teachers, did we teach well and who not so well?

✓ What did we teach well and not so well as a result of the professional learning experience?

✓ Where specifically are the gaps in teacher learning, where are the strengths, what was learned, and what has still to be learned?

✓ How do we develop a collective understanding of progress among teachers in the school?

✓ What are examples of the short-cycle formative assessment strategies leaders are utilizing on a regular basis that provide evidence of impact?

In other words, the concept of assessment as feedback for leaders works on the same level that "assessment as feedback for teachers" does (Hattie, 2012a, p. 163), with leaders also needing feedback about their effects on each teacher.

TOP 5: Engaging in Dialogue Not Monologue

Leaders understand the power of engaging in active listening. Listening to others' learning is not just a teaching need (Hattie, 2012a); it is also a principal need. In other words, just as teachers need to listen to students thinking aloud about their learning, principals need to suspend judgment of teacher practices in order to listen to teachers. This process can allow principals to learn how to operationalize the theories of practice by systematically and effectively using high-impact deliberate interventions that they are acquiring from professional learning opportunities. Such strategies might include posing well-crafted open-ended questions that cause teachers to reflect on their practices, using the results of teachers' self-assessments on high-impact instructional practices to inform next steps, and creating collaborative structures within the school day (i.e., professional learning communities) for teachers to come together and collectively reflect on their impact on learning.

This idea underscores Hattie's (2009) personal discovery that feedback is most powerful when it occurs "from the student to the teacher" (p. 173). Similarly, we propose that the most powerful form of feedback among teachers and principals occurs when it is from the teacher to the principal. In other words, when principals seek, or at least are open to, feedback from teachers as to what teachers know, what they understand, where they make errors, when they have misconceptions, when they are not effectively utilizing the professional learning, "then teaching and learning can be synchronized and powerful" (Hattie, 2009, p. 173) for the adults in the school. More importantly, leaders who engage in active listening build rapport as well as relationships with teachers, build "teacher voice" into leadership, expose the knowledge that teachers bring to learning, and allow the leader to determine the degree to which teachers are achieving the learning intentions and meeting the success criteria so that adjustments in leadership can be made. Critical questions that leaders might be asking themselves in this particular theory of practice are shown in Figure 2.6.

TOP 6: Embracing the Challenge

Leaders recognize that classroom as well as school life is a challenge for most students, teachers, and leaders and that they need to accept, embrace, and shape the challenge to what they want it to be. In other words, the art of leading is recognizing that what is challenging to one

Figure 2.6   Critical Questions for Engaging in Dialogue Not Monologue

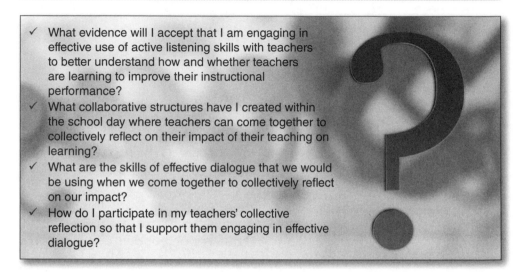

✓ What evidence will I accept that I am engaging in effective use of active listening skills with teachers to better understand how and whether teachers are learning to improve their instructional performance?

✓ What collaborative structures have I created within the school day where teachers can come together to collectively reflect on their impact of their teaching on learning?

✓ What are the skills of effective dialogue that we would be using when we come together to collectively reflect on our impact?

✓ How do I participate in my teachers' collective reflection so that I support them engaging in effective dialogue?

teacher may not be challenging to another teacher. Consequently, leaders must pay constant attention to the particularized differences inherent in their staff and pursue collective opportunities so that teachers can work together with the principal and other teachers to make the difference. Specifically, the leader's role is to decide on how to enlist teachers in the challenge of the learning.

Essential to engaging teachers in the challenge of learning is the development of clear learning intentions and success criteria. On the student side of the equation, the use of learning intentions and success criteria is a necessary part of the learning journey because, "when students understand these, they can see the purposes of the challenges that are so critical to success in learning" (Hattie, 2012a, p. 164). Likewise, when leaders make clear the learning intentions and success criteria for teachers, they, just like their students, can see the reasons of the challenge essential to their success in learning. For example, when the principal along with his or her teachers formulates clear professional learning goals such as "75% of teachers will be proficiently implementing effective feedback by June 2016 as measured by a school-based rubric with quarterly monitoring throughout the year," they not only direct attention toward goal-relevant behaviors, encourage teacher effort, increase teacher persistence, and motivate teachers to apply strategies to assist with goal attainment (Locke & Latham, 2002), but they also help teachers to see the purposes of the challenge that are so critical to success in learning. Critical questions that leaders might be asking themselves in this particular theory of practice are reflected in Figure 2.7.

Figure 2.7   Critical Questions for Embracing the Challenge

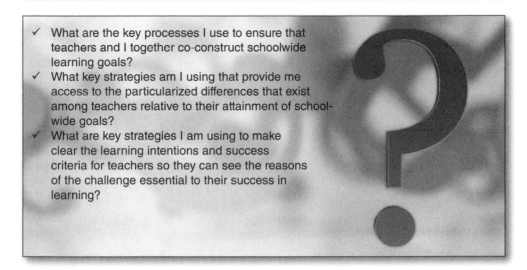

✓ What are the key processes I use to ensure that teachers and I together co-construct schoolwide learning goals?

✓ What key strategies am I using that provide me access to the particularized differences that exist among teachers relative to their attainment of school-wide goals?

✓ What are key strategies I am using to make clear the learning intentions and success criteria for teachers so they can see the reasons of the challenge essential to their success in learning?

TOP 7: Developing Relational Trust

Leaders highly regard their role in developing relational trust within class-rooms and throughout the school. Why? Because there is persuasive evidence that level of trust among members of a school community and the way in which the members work together is linked to the level of social and academic progress of students (Bryk & Schneider, 2002). In short, as the level of trust among staff members grows, the social and academic progress of students increases. Another reason why developing warm, trustworthy, empathetic school and classroom climates is so important is to recognize that teacher and leader learning, just like student learning, thrive on error. The major reason is to allow teachers and leaders to feel okay about making mistakes and not knowing and to establish a climate in which we welcome error as a learning opportunity.

Leaders create such a climate and build relational trust by displaying and expecting from others the four qualities on which such trust is based (Bryk & Schneider, 2002). The first and perhaps the most fundamental of these qualities is respect. Leaders demonstrate respect by valuing the ideas of other people, which means that they practice active listening and are open to influence. It also means that they have firmly established through-out the school, and have supported through ongoing professional devel-opment, the skills required for effective dialogue (Theory of Practice 5) during interactions as a staff. Second, leaders gain trust by applying the wisdom from historical leaders such as President Woodrow Wilson when he said, "The ear of the leader must ring with the voices of the people" and the guidance from a placard supposedly sitting in President Lyndon

Baines Johnson's office saying "You ain't learnin' nothin' when you're doin' all the talkin'." Effective leaders employ deep listening skills designed to understand others' assumptions and points of view.

Capability is the third quality on which others' judgment of trust is based. When teachers are dependent on leaders to succeed in the work of educating children, they care deeply about their capability or the lack thereof. For example, Bryk and Schneider (2002) pointed out that teachers, parents, and non-parent community members are quick to criticize a leader's competence when the school culture is not safe and orderly or when the individuals who work within that environment interact in a disrespectful manner. Many times, a leader's capability comes into question based on the manner in which he or she deals with observed incidents of incompetence among his or her staff. Hence, it is imperative that leaders bolster teachers' commitment by tackling perceived breaches in school norms of practice and/or behaviors in others that work to undermine the school's collective efforts.

The last quality of trust is integrity. The first question we ask is, "Can we trust the leader to keep his or her word?" Simply put, when individuals perceive that a leader's words are incongruent with his or her actions or when leaders do not settle disagreements arising out of competing individual interests within a school community in a compassionate and impartial manner, staff members come to distrust that leader. In brief, "when all is said and done, actions [of leaders] must be understood as advancing the best interests of children" (Bryk & Schneider, 2002, p. 26).

There are a number of important benefits to leaders as they scale relational trust. To begin with, strong relational trust between leaders and teachers makes it more likely that reform initiatives will be implemented deeply throughout the school because trust reduces the sense of risk associated with the change in practice. When teachers and school leaders trust one another and sense support from parents, they feel safe to experiment with new practices. Likewise, relational trust promotes the necessary social exchanges among faculty members as they learn from one another by engaging in "open to learning conversations" (Robinson, 2011, p. 40) with colleagues about what is working and what is not, which means exposing your own ignorance and making yourself vulnerable. Without trust, genuine conversations of this sort remain highly unlikely. Moreover, relational trust supports a moral imperative to take on the difficult work of school improvement (Fullan, 2003). Critical questions that leaders might be asking themselves about developing relational trust are depicted in Figure 2.8.

TOP 8: Teaching the Academic Vocabulary of Learning

Leaders recognize that the research overwhelmingly demonstrates that parent involvement in children's learning is positively related to increases in student achievement (Henderson & Mapp, 2002). However, many parents

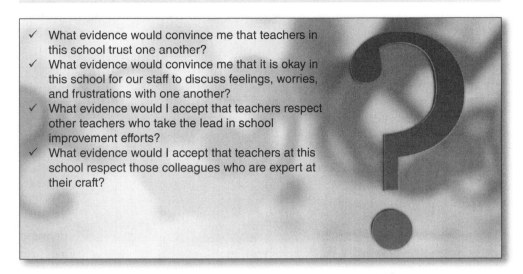

Figure 2.8   Critical Questions for Developing Relational Trust

✓ What evidence would convince me that teachers in this school trust one another?

✓ What evidence would convince me that it is okay in this school for our staff to discuss feelings, worries, and frustrations with one another?

✓ What evidence would I accept that teachers respect other teachers who take the lead in school improvement efforts?

✓ What evidence would I accept that teachers at this school respect those colleagues who are expert at their craft?

do not see schools as friendly places and are not conversant with much of the educational jargon used by school personnel. Overcoming this barrier and thereby capitalizing on the many positive benefits of parent involvement requires school leaders to take very deliberate steps to teach parents the importance of such concepts as "deliberate practice, concentration, the difference between surface and deep knowing, and the nature of learning intentions and success criteria" (Hattie, 2012a, p. 165). That is, leaders along with their teachers must help parents to understand the academic vocabulary of learning being used within the school.

Leaders must be well organized in their approach to engage parent participation in school, as investigators have identified a lack of planning and a lack of mutual understanding as the two greatest barriers to effective parent involvement (Epstein, 2010). For example, leaders should consider offering parents a variety of roles in the context of a well-organized and long-lasting program by providing opportunities for parents to choose from a range of activities that accommodate different schedules, preferences, and capabilities and by communicating to parents that their involvement and support, regardless of their own level of education, has a positive impact on their children's performance in school. Because parent involvement tends to wane as their children grow older, secondary leaders must provide parents different forms of participation from their elementary colleagues—e.g., monitoring homework, helping students make post-secondary plans and select courses that support these plans, parent-school agreements on rewards for achievement and behavioral improvements— as well as some of the "standby" functions such as regular home-school communication about student progress and parent attendance at school-sponsored activities.

Regardless of the level of school, parent programs that include a focus on parent involvement in instruction—e.g., by conducting learning activities in the home that are aligned with teachers' established learning intentions and success criteria, assisting with homework, and monitoring and encouraging the learning activities of older students—must be developed by leaders. Last, leaders must make a special effort to engage the involvement of parents of disadvantaged students, who perhaps stand to benefit the most from parent participation in their learning but whose parents are often initially reluctant to become involved. Critical questions that leaders might be asking themselves in this particular theory of practice include, but are not limited to, those within Figure 2.9.

Figure 2.9   Critical Questions for Teaching the Academic Vocabulary of Learning

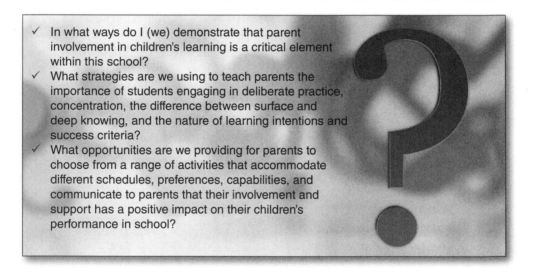

✓ In what ways do I (we) demonstrate that parent involvement in children's learning is a critical element within this school?
✓ What strategies are we using to teach parents the importance of students engaging in deliberate practice, concentration, the difference between surface and deep knowing, and the nature of learning intentions and success criteria?
✓ What opportunities are we providing for parents to choose from a range of activities that accommodate different schedules, preferences, capabilities, and communicate to parents that their involvement and support has a positive impact on their children's performance in school?

TOP 9: Reinforcing That Learning and Leading Is Hard Work

Leaders know all too well and appreciate the fact that learning is not always an enjoyable and easy endeavor. Often, learning is a messy, frustrating, nonlinear, recursive process that at times causes the learner to operate at a variety of levels of the knowledge continuum, co-constructing and reconstructing knowledge and ideas with others as they wrestle with challenging problems. The good news is, grappling with educational problems is not a new phenomenon to American educators. For example, with the passage in 1920 of the Nineteenth Amendment to the Constitution, which established voting rights for women, public educators realized that curriculum modifications were needed to ensure that all students, not just male students, obtained the reading, writing, and computational skills that they would need to effectively participate in American society. Now, fast forward to our present challenges, spurred on by Common Core State Standards that require a number of fundamental shifts in teachers' instructional practice (i.e., cross-content literacy expectations, etc.).

Consequently, leaders must create and nurture a school environment in which error is not only tolerated but, more importantly, is welcomed and celebrated, thereby communicating to teachers that they can be secure in their role as practicing learners, similar to a practicing physician or a practicing attorney, to confidently "learn, re-learn, and explore knowledge and understanding" (Hattie, 2012a, p. 19). In short, learning is hard work and requires a great deal of concentration, persistence, and commitment to seek out the next additional challenging task. Critical questions that leaders might be asking themselves in this particular theory of practice are reflected in Figure 2.10.

Figure 2.10   Critical Questions for Reinforcing That Learning Is Hard Work

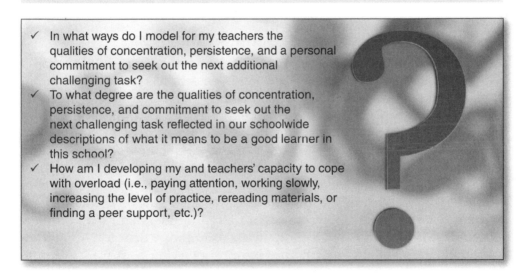

✓ In what ways do I model for my teachers the qualities of concentration, persistence, and a personal commitment to seek out the next additional challenging task?
✓ To what degree are the qualities of concentration, persistence, and commitment to seek out the next challenging task reflected in our schoolwide descriptions of what it means to be a good learner in this school?
✓ How am I developing my and teachers' capacity to cope with overload (i.e., paying attention, working slowly, increasing the level of practice, rereading materials, or finding a peer support, etc.)?

FIVE ELEMENTS OF INSTRUCTIONAL LEADERSHIP ABILITY

Inasmuch as school leaders often feel compelled to wear many hats and are pulled in many different directions simultaneously—in one moment, a politician; in another, an instructional leader; in another, a public relations director; in another, a mayor of a small city; and in yet another, a small-business manager—a unifying thread runs through the entire leadership framework to provide a coherent architecture. In light of the stress produced from the multiple competing leadership roles, the unifying thread, not unlike the thread that binds together many heavy goods that must withstand considerable stresses, such as upholstery, car seating, tarpaulins, tents, and parachutes, require strong threads. In this case, the strong unifying thread that weaves together the fabric of these five elements of instructional leadership ability consists of nine tightly twisted fibers or theories of practice that require teachers and leaders to think in specific ways about their roles. All of the components of the framework serve this primary purpose. In helping teachers to understanding the impact that they are having on student learning, a leader creates a web of connectivity and collaboration whereby it is easy for leaders and teachers to interface with each other and tap into the organization's knowledge base—that is, its collective brain—to resolve problems, to activate collaborative effort, and to encourage knowledge sharing and information exchange. That is, they create a powerful web of informed coordinated effort!

Each of the five elements of the framework refers to a distinct aspect of instructional leadership ability. The elements form a coherent body of knowledge and skill and are briefly described below; subsequent chapters will provide much greater detail.

Establishing a Shared Vision/Mission, Goals, and Expectations

Leadership impacts student achievement through its emphasis on shared values and clear academic and learning expectations. The work environment of most schools today is characterized by multiple conflicting demands that tend to make everything seem equally important; thus, clearly articulating the school's learning intentions (goals) distinguishes what is most important from what is least important and focuses staff and student attention and effort accordingly. The importance of high relational trust in this leadership element is evident in that leaders who give more emphasis to co-creating and communicating learning intentions and shared expectations, helping the community to understand the academic vocabulary of learning, and informing the community of academic accomplishments are hallmarks of higher performing schools. Another feature that distinguishes higher from lower performing schools is the cultivation of teacher buy-in and commitment (Bryk, 2010). In schools with high student achievement or high gains in student achievement, the school's strategic priorities are clearly communicated by leaders at the same time that they are reflected in school and classroom routines and procedures. That is, highly successful leaders drive school change by nurturing trusting relationships and by structuring the way in which teachers do their work.

Strategic Resourcing

The use of the word "strategic" indicates that this leadership element is about the deliberate practice of securing and allocating time, money, and people—precious resources that are aligned with and used to support attainment of the prioritized school goals—rather than the leadership skill in securing resources per se. In other words, the reader should not inter-pret this leadership practice as demonstrating skill in acquiring additional funds, resources, and/or materials through such means as business dona-tions, fundraising, grant writing, and so on, as these practices do not necessarily serve the planned purposes of the school. Therefore, strategic resourcing is about how effectively the leader uses the available resources to accomplish its most important priorities.

Ensuring Teacher and Staff Effectiveness

This leadership element makes a strong impact on student achievement (Robinson, 2011) and involves the orchestration of four leadership actions: (1) engaging faculty members in an ongoing dialogue about instructional practices and the effect that these practices are having on student learning; (2) collaborating with faculty members to coordinate and review the school's curriculum, i.e., developing clearly articulated learning progressions in the teaching of reading across all grade levels; (3) providing feedback to and securing feedback from teachers as a result of frequent classroom observations that help them to answer the question, "Where to next?" in relation to identified learning intentions; and (4) monitoring student progress numerous times throughout the year for the purpose of classroom, grade level, and/or department improvement.

Leading and Participating in Teacher/ Leader Learning and Development

This leadership element involves the leader in two simultaneous roles—promoting and participating in teacher development. This professional development in which teachers and leaders engage includes both formal learning opportunities (i.e., scheduled staff development throughout the year) as well as informal learning opportunities (i.e., planning period dialogue). This leadership element has a strong impact on school performance (Robinson, 2011). In high-achieving schools, teachers report that the school principal is actively engaged in teachers' learning. Leaders of high-achieving schools have an acute awareness of teaching and learning in their schools, so they know first-hand what direct instructional support their teachers require (Seashore-Louis, Leithwood, Wahlstrom, & Anderson, 2010). Leaders in high-achieving schools, con-trary to those in low-performing schools, tend to host the conversation about teaching and learning and also tend to participate in staff discus-sion of teaching problems. Teachers in high-achieving schools tend to report that the principal is a source of instructional advice, which implies that the principal is both accessible and knowledgeable about instructional matters.

Providing an Orderly, Safe, and Supportive Environment

This leadership element describes leadership practices that ensure that leaders, teachers, and students can focus on teaching and learning and are not distracted from this primary focus. Leadership at high-achieving schools is characterized by an emphasis on and success in establishing an orderly and safe and school environment through clear and consistently enforced behavioral expectations and discipline codes. Teachers in high-performing schools report that the principal is effective in buffering them from undue pressure from education officials and from parents (Bryk, 2010). Last, an orderly and safe environment is also one in which the leader addresses staff conflict quickly and effectively.

FOUR LEVELS OF LEADERSHIP PERFORMANCE

Five sets of rubrics, one for each instructional leadership element, are used to guide the rating performance of instructional leadership ability. Levels of performance are typically divided into 3- to 6-point scales and are given labels such as Basic, Proficient, or Advanced; Needs Improvement, Meets Expectations, or Exceeds Expectations; Seldom, Sometimes, Usually, or Often; Poor, Good, Excellent, or Superior, etc. We have selected to use a 4-point level of performance that includes four labels: Exemplary, Proficient, Progressing, and Not Meeting Expectations. The rubric for a particular level describes the performance outcome at that level, and each subsequent rubric describes the quality

Figure 2.11   Generic Descriptions of Four Levels of Leadership Performance

Exemplary	Proficient	Progressing	Not Meeting Expectations
The impact of leader's actions help others within the district/school apply the nine Theories of Practice—powerful behaviors, ways of thinking—to their actions, thereby increasing leadership capacity within the district/school.	The impact of leader's actions is both adequate, necessary, and meets the school needs. Actions relevant to this element are appropriate reflections of quality work with only normal variations.	The impact of leader's actions reflects performance that shows potential but lacks sufficient proficiencies to improve student learning, instructional practice, and/or other responsibilities.	The impact of leader's actions demonstrate that the leader either does not understand what is required for proficiency or has demonstrated through his or her action or inaction that he or she chooses not to work toward proficiency.

of performance at each subsequent level. A generic description of each of the four performance levels used within the instructional leadership evaluation is offered in Figure 2.11.

Exemplary Leadership Performance

Leadership performance at the exemplary level not only includes all of the requirements for the proficient level but also goes far beyond those expectations and thus has an impact on an entire organization (i.e., school district). Exemplary leadership eclipses proficient leadership in terms of its impact on students, staff members, parents, and the school district as a whole (i.e., it results in system-wide impact). Exemplary leaders help every other element within the organization (i.e., the school district for a principal and the entire school for assistant principals) to become as good as they are (Reeves, 2009). In other words, exemplary leaders are not merely successful at their own roles within their own building. That sort of performance is to be expected, is proficient, and reflects the majority of leadership performance. Rather, exemplary leaders take great pride in helping others within the district to apply the theories of practice, thereby

Figure 2.12   Exemplary Performance Real-World Examples

Example	Real-World *Exemplary* Performance
1	The principal serves as a classroom observation/feedback mentor to at least one other principal in the system and has created objective evidence that the other principal's classroom observation/feedback skills have improved based on that principal's assessment on the instructional leadership ability framework.
2	The leader has coached at least one other principal in other schools to improve his or her data-analysis skills in order to inform instructional decision-making and has created objective evidence that the other principal's data-analysis and decision-making skills have improved based on that principal's assessment on the instructional leadership ability framework.
3	The leader monitors teachers' implementation of various initiatives, tracks the impact of these initiatives on student growth, and shares effective/ineffective practices and impacts with other school leaders.
4	The leader routinely shares professional learning opportunities from his or her own action research with other schools, departments, districts, and organizations.
5	The leader creates high-quality collaborative opportunities for teachers to improve their teaching of what it is that their students are supposed to learn and serves as a mentor to at least one other principal within the district to improve their skills to lead teacher learning and development.

increasing leadership capacity within the organization. Some real-world exemplary leadership practices that help others become more capable in the area of instructional leadership ability are reflected in Figure 2.12.

Proficient Leadership Performance

Proficient leadership performance is adequate, necessary, and meets organizational needs. Inasmuch as exemplary performance demonstrates system-wide impact, proficient performance reflects local impact (i.e., within the school). The vast majority of leaders within an effective school district are proficient. Examples of leadership practices that are performed at the Proficient level (adequate, necessary, and clearly makes a significant contribution to the school) within the instructional leadership ability criterion might include practices that are reflected in Figure 2.13.

Given the human tendency to view any performance short of "Exemplary" as being mediocre, the more clearly and rigorously we define proficient performance, the more remarkable the practice of the genuinely

Figure 2.13   Proficient Performance Real-World Examples

Example	Real-World *Proficient* Performance
1	The leader has effectively implemented a system for collecting feedback from teachers as to what they know, what they understand, where they make errors, and when they have misconceptions about use of high-impact instructional practices.
2	In addition to the formal feedback that is consistent with the district evaluation system indicators, the leader provides recurring informal feedback on high-effect-size strategies to reinforce proficient performance and highlight the strengths of colleagues and staff. Both the leader and employees can cite examples of where feedback on high-effect-size strategies is used to improve individual and organizational performance.
3	The leader provides and at times leads recurring opportunities for professional learning for individual and collegial groups focused on issues directly related to prioritized school targets and faculty proficiency at high-effect-size strategies and student learning needs.
4	The leader's approach to professional learning includes a plan for the implementation of the prioritized instructional needs (e.g., use of research-based, high-impact instructional practices, data analysis, effective use of instructional technology that serves to produce new learning, use of culturally relevant practices) aligned to school improvement plan, and some effort has been made to differentiate (e.g., utilizing coaching, mentoring, collaborative teams) support and embed professional development to meet the needs of all faculty members. The leader is able to use data from the evaluation of instructional personnel to assess proficiencies and identify priority needs to support and retain proficient and exemplary faculty members.

exemplary leadership will become. Specifically, the "Proficient" level describes leadership performance that has local impact (i.e., within the school) and meets organizational needs. It is adequate, necessary, and clearly makes a significant contribution to the school. Typically, the majority of school leaders will be in the Proficient level once they have a clear understanding of what the framework requires and have made the adjustments and growth necessary to upgrade performance. More importantly, the label of proficient performance will take on new significance when it is consistently related to all members within the organization, from the boardroom to the classroom, for performance describing the challenging requirements for proficient leadership performance.

Progressing Leadership Performance

Leadership performance at this level generally reflects performance that shows potential but lacks sufficient proficiencies to improve student learning, instructional practice, and/or other responsibilities. The leader understands what is required for success, is willing to work toward that goal, and, with coaching and support, can become proficient within a reasonable time frame. In each of the previous two performance levels, we have stressed the importance of providing clearly worded, jargon-free "word pictures" of leadership performance. The value of clarity is even more important when describing progressing leadership performance. Why? Because in our review of principal-evaluation documents, we have found that one of the most challenging elements of dealing with progressing performance is that it is poorly worded. Take for instance this description of progressing leadership practice: "Occasionally passes along interesting articles and ideas to colleagues." Even when describing leadership that is not yet proficient (progressing leadership performance), the issue should not be the frequency with which the leader provides information to staff, but rather whether the information is aligned with school goals, is of sufficient quality to be understood, and whether the information is used to make good decisions to improve student achievement. Consequently, a less ambiguous, more accurate description of progressing leadership performance may then look something like this: "While the leader makes certain that staff receive interesting educational articles and ideas, these articles may not be aligned with school performance or learning goals and are not necessarily used to improve instructional practices." Clearly worded documents will help both the person being evaluated to engage in more accurate self-assessments and the evaluator to engage in courageous conversations where performance that is not proficient is identified without equivocation.

Figure 2.14 provides examples of descriptions of progressing leadership performance in the area of instructional leadership ability.

Figure 2.14   Progressing Performance Real-World Examples

Example	Real-World Progressing Performance
1	The leader is aware of the differentiated needs of faculty and staff members, but professional development is only embedded in faculty meetings, without the incorporation of collaboration, study teams, etc., to meet the unique needs of staff.
2	Leadership monitoring of professional learning is focused primarily on faculty participation, with minimal attention being given to the impact of instructional proficiency on student learning.
3	The leader tends to view feedback as a linear process—i.e., something that the leader provides teachers rather than a two-way communication whereby the leader also learns from the teachers' perceived expertise and uses such data to provide the necessary support.

Not Meeting Expectations

The last leadership performance level, Not Meeting Expectations, describes leaders who do not understand what is required for proficiency or who have demonstrated through their action or inaction that they choose not to work toward proficiency. Not Meeting Expectations leadership performance is clearly inadequate, unacceptable, and poses a potential threat to the organization and the people within it. Again, the need for clear wording is absolutely critical. Some examples of leadership performance at this level within the criterion instructional leadership ability are reflected in Figure 2.15.

The four levels of leadership performance are especially useful when the instructional leadership elements are used for supervision and evaluation. However, even when they are employed by individual leaders to

Figure 2.15   Not Meeting Expectations Performance Real-World Examples

Example	Real-World Not Meeting Expectations Performance
1	There is no or only minimal monitoring of teachers that results in feedback on instructional proficiency.
2	The leader is not aware of the high-effect-size strategies that need to be implemented by teachers or fails to clearly communicate them to faculty. Consequently, feedback on high-effect-size strategies is rare, nonspecific, and not constructive.
3	The leader fails to adequately support district and state-mandated initiatives with specific plans, actions, feedback, or monitoring.

create internal feedback resources that assist with self-appraisal and self-assessment, they serve as potent resources for effective learners. Hattie and Timperley (2007) suggested that leaders must function as students of their own effects by utilizing the metacognitive skills of self-assessment, a "self-regulatory proficiency that is powerful in selecting and interpreting information in ways that provide feedback" (p. 94) to the individual as to next steps or to support mentoring or coaching relationships, as they serve to inform a professional discussion of leadership practices and suggest areas for further growth.

SUMMARY

This chapter identified nine theories of practice—individual and organizational beliefs requiring changes in how both teachers and leaders should view their roles and actions that, when applied to their practice, enhance student performance. The theories of practice form a unifying thread that runs through the entire framework to provide the architecture of the evaluation framework. The nine theories of practice support the elements of instructional leadership ability, which clearly describe the prioritized actions of school leaders that research suggests leads to increased student achievement. Next, we identified five elements of the framework that refer to a distinct aspect of instructional leadership ability. These five elements form a coherent body of knowledge and skill. Last, we described the four levels of leadership performance, which we have built into the model and are used to guide the rating performance of instructional leadership ability.

The next chapter, entitled "Element 1: Establishing a Shared Vision/Mission, Goals and Expectations," describes the first of five instructional leadership performance elements that make up the framework for instructional leadership ability.

Element 1: Establishing a Shared Vision/ Mission, Goals, and Expectations

The power of setting goals, the first of five elements of instructional leadership ability, is grounded in a long tradition of social psychology research (Latham & Locke, 2006). In fact, goal-setting theory is generally accepted as among the most valid and useful motivation theories in industrial and organizational psychology, human resource management, and organizational behavior. Hundreds of studies that have been conducted in numerous countries and contexts have consistently demonstrated that setting specific, challenging goals can powerfully drive behavior and boost performance.

RATIONALE AND DESCRIPTION

With the ever-increasing demands for greater accountability and a plethora of competing initiatives, it is easy for those in schools to experience overload, fragmentation, and incoherence. Highly effective school leaders understand that one of the ways that they can reduce the feeling of overload and fragmentation and promote coherence is by setting and communicating clear goals and expectations. When clear goals are set, leaders unequivocally communicate the importance of prioritized areas of collective focus over other issues of lesser importance.

In their summary of 35 years of empirical research on goal-setting theory, Locke and Latham (2002) found that goal setting affects achievement through a number of purposes and processes. To begin with, goals have a directive purpose that helps an individual as well as the collectivity to direct attention and effort toward goal-relevant tasks and activities. That is, clearly stated priority goals tend to cause all stakeholders to rally around a higher purpose that has meaning for individuals as well as the collective whole. Second, goals can have an energizing capacity. When people are committed to a goal, they are motivated to engage in persistent goal-relevant behavior. Third, goals impact persistence in that one's increased attention and effort leads to better enjoyment of and performance in the relevant task or activity. Fourth, goals lead to the task-relevant knowledge and skills that are required for goal attainment. Last, goals create a discrepancy between the current state and the desired state and serve to motivate the individual to reduce the gap that separates the two states.

Goal setting is the first of five elements of instructional leadership ability and has, on average, a moderate impact on student outcomes (Robinson, Lloyd, & Rowe, 2008) or an effect size of 0.42. With an effect size of 0.42, the practice of establishing goals and expectations surpasses what Hattie (2009) refers to as the "hinge point" (p. 16), or a 0.40 effect size, which is the threshold above which all teachers and leaders should be aspiring to demonstrate. In other words, the impact on student learning that this leadership practice yields is approximately a year's worth of academic growth. But, how exactly does the setting of goals and expectations actually work? Simply put, this element works indirectly by focusing and directing the work of educators around promoting learning and achievement on the part of students.

Goal-setting activities include such actions as determining what goals to set, securing the commitment of all those who are responsible for achieving the goals, and communicating the goals to all interested stakeholders (both internal and external). It is important to point out, however, that "the quality of goal setting cannot be separated from the quality of relationships" (Robinson, 2011, p. 45). In other words, leaders can certainly set clearly stated priority goals, but absent the use of principled motivational strategies aimed at those whose efforts are needed in order to achieve them, the stated goals will remain hollow words.

Consequently, leaders can either reap the benefits of goal setting or they can fall prey to the pitfalls of goal setting. The choice is theirs. Leaders choosing the former over the latter would be wise to pay close attention to the research of Latham and Locke (2006), who pointed out that three conditions need to be in place in order to take advantage of the considerable potential benefits of goal setting for teachers and students (as well as principals and central office administrators). To begin with, people need to feel personally committed to the goal. People do not commit to goals that they do not believe are important. Therefore, leaders need to help people see how the collective goals are mutually advantageous and support what they individually value. Mutually advantageous goals result when leaders provide others with an opportunity to achieve what is valued and when they have helped others to accept that the current state is woefully insufficient compared with the desired state to warrant pursuit of the goal. This is very much a relational process whereby leaders cause others to discover the power of allegiance, which leads to a genuine collective responsibility with full commitment to the cause. Toward that end, leaders must not only spend time listening to others but also practice deep listening to others as they express their own values and commitments and engage in collaborative problem solving, which usually emerges through dialogue and not monologue. In addition to nurturing a collective versus a singular point of view, leaders also must help others understand that what they now have falls sufficiently short of what they truly want. This requires leaders to engage in "constructive problem talk" (Robinson, 2011, p. 50), whereby leaders work alongside others to identify, describe, and analyze problems in a way that contributes to a "we-we solution" (Fullan, 2008, p. 49), avoids blame, and offers a collaborative approach to improvement.

Next, people must have confidence in their capacity to achieve the goals to which they are committed. Nothing undermines the power of goal setting more than leaders who develop goals without having first considered for example teachers' capacity for achieving them. Consequently, Robinson (2011) maintained that if "the responsible system" (p. 52) finds itself deficient in the capacity to achieve a particular goal, leaders would be well advised to initially set a learning goal rather than a performance goal. Performance goals are about the achievement of a specific outcome, such as increasing student nonfiction writing achievement by a certain percentage or raising the number of schools within the district that have proficiently implemented professional learning communities. When establishing a performance goal, one assumes that those who are responsible for achieving the goal possess the requested skills and abilities needed to achieve the goal. Conversely, learning goals tend to focus on the knowledge and skills that people need in order to accomplish a specific performance goal. For instance, one of the expectations within the Common Core State Standards (CCSS) is that instruction in reading, writing, speaking, listening, and language be a shared responsibility within the school. In other words, with the inclusion in the English Language Arts CCSS of disciplinary literacy concepts for reading, students will be able to read like a mathematician, historian, scientist, literary critic, or musician—whatever is required throughout school. Thus, it makes sense that schools across the nation will be providing professional development training for all teachers in how to teach reading strategies within all content areas. What does not make sense, however, is to set a new performance goal (for example, "80% of students will meet the standard in reading by a certain date") when it is clear that teachers are not clear as to the strategies, processes, or procedures to teach reading. Considering teachers' capacity to teach reading, it would be much more productive to set a learning goal that requires inquiry into how to teach reading within all content areas. Through careful examination of the learning culture and the size of gap that exists between the current level of performance and the amount and type of work that it would take to elevate that performance to proposed and/or needed goal levels, leaders will come to know whether to set learning or performance goals.

Last, the goal must be stated in specific terms so that people can monitor their progress toward the goal. Any credible organization must have clear goals and a way to know at a given moment whether it is on track to achieving them. According to Barber, Moffit, and Kihn (2011) "good targets are defined by five characteristics that comprise the SMART framework" (p. 91). The authors then proceed to describe the acronym with which most of us are very familiar, with one important difference. Most likely, you recall that the "S" indicates that the goal is *specific* (that is, its meaning and implications are clear, so it leaves no one guessing as to the target) and the "M" indicates that the goal is *measurable* (that is, it has both a baseline as well as a projected gain measure). It is the "A," however, that is significantly different from other similar acronyms. You might think that the "A" means achievable or attainable. Instead, the "A" stands for *ambitious*, indicating that the goal should reflect a stretch from the existing to the desired level of performance so that it inspires others to new challenges. The remaining portions of the acronym are consistent with the more popular versions—"R" stands for *realistic* (indicating that the goal is grounded in factors over which the school has control and influence), and the "T" stands for *time limited* (indicating that the goal has a defined deadline both to ensure accountability and to establish a sense of urgency). In our work with Cognition Education (a highly successful professional learning and development firm in New Zealand, whose purpose is to design intervention platforms worldwide that improve the instructional and evaluative skills of teachers, the professional leadership and analytical skills of principals, and the implementation skills of policy makers) and our training in Visible Learning[plus] (the application of Professor John Hattie's well-known Visible Learning research) we have added two additional letters to the SMART acronym: "E" and "R." The "E" in the newly minted acronym *SMART+ER goal* refers to *evaluation*, as goals cannot simply be set without evaluating whether or not progress is being made toward goal attainment. The "R" in the acronym refers to *reevaluation* as goals must be continuously reevaluated over the course of the year (we suggest at minimum four times a year). In other words, the regularity of the review will help everyone within the organization keep a sharp focus on the goal. Hence, the importance of setting SMART+ER goals is to establish a metric, time, and place when the outcomes are achieved, evaluated, and reevaluated.

Conversely, just as leaders can benefit from the important potential of setting goals and expectations, leaders also can be the victims of goal-setting misuse. So what are the common challenges to goal setting, and what might be some key strategies for overcoming the challenges? For example, in many cases, leaders set too many goals, which increases stress within a school and perpetuates a sense of fragmentation and incoherence. A commonsense strategy for overcoming this pitfall might be to prioritize target areas and to set no more than two or three clear SMART+ER goals on which to focus improvement efforts. In other cases, individuals within the system possess inadequate skills and knowledge to achieve the goals that leaders have set. As stated earlier, when it is clear that teachers possess insufficient knowledge and skills to bring about the desired improvements in student performance, leaders would be wise to create related learning goals versus performance goals. For instance, schools implementing the Common Core State Standards understand that all teachers assume a responsibility for teaching reading and writing. However, most teachers are ill prepared to be teachers of reading within their content area. With this in mind, it makes little sense for leaders and their staff to set a new performance goal, such as "75% percent of students at a particular grade level will meet and/or exceed the standard in reading comprehension" (i.e., reading closely to determine what the text says explicitly and making logical inferences from it, etc.), knowing that teachers and most likely building leaders do not know how to reach the reading goal. Rather, it makes more sense to establish a clear learning goal, such as "80% of staff will implement at the proficient and higher levels the reading strategies learned during professional learning events by the end of the year." Thus, learning goals give teachers time and opportunity to learn how to do the work that the performance goal requires.

EVIDENCE OF IMPACT

Leaders provide evidence of their evolving knowledge and skill in the area of setting goals and expectations by developing deliberate practice and school-improvement plans and by applying new learning gained from participating in professional learning activities. Some examples of how leaders can demonstrate evidence of impact in this leadership element follow:

- There is agreement in this school among teachers and administrators about the importance of the current learning and/or performance goals.

- Learning and/or performance goals in this school have been prioritized to reflect the two or three most important improvement needs.
- The alignment between overarching school goals and the goals set by content area/grade level leaders is clear and well understood.
- Teachers are clear about the learning goals for which they are responsible.
- Teachers feel personally committed to achieving the goals for which they are responsible.
- Teachers possess or have confidence that they will acquire the knowledge and skills that are needed to achieve the goals for which they are responsible.
- Teachers have access to the resources (i.e., professional learning, time, support, and feedback) that are needed to achieve the goals for which they are responsible.

SUMMARY

In summary, setting goals influences the details on which educational practitioners choose to focus and act. However, the skill of setting quality goals and the skill of building quality relationships between leaders and staff are inseparable concepts because, in the absence of motivation to achieve them, such goals remain hollow words. Goals regulate the actions of adults by focusing attention on goal-relevant behavior. Second, goals affect the intensity of individuals' actions—and their related emotions—depending on the importance that individuals attach to their goals. The more difficult a valued goal is, the more intense the efforts are to attain it and the more success that is experienced following its attainment. Third, a valued goal affects peoples' persistence. Committed people do not quit until the goal is attained. Fourth, goals encourage people to search for task-relevant knowledge. Finally, goal effectiveness is based on context factors; thus, while goals have considerable potential benefits, they also have potential pitfalls. With sufficient foresight, however, these potential problems can be overcome or prevented.

Figure 3.1 depicts the rubric for Element 1: Establishing Shared Vision/Mission, Goals, and Expectations. It consists of three sections. First, we provide rich "word descriptions" of leadership practice that are situated along a continuum ranging from exemplary on one end to not meeting expectations on the other. Next, we identify the critical attributes of the element. That is, the critical attributes provide essential guidance for observers as well as those being evaluated in distinguishing between practices at adjacent levels of leadership performance. These attributes are very instrumental in training and in the actual work of self-assessment, observation, and evaluation. Last, we present possible real-world examples of what the instructional leadership practice looks like according to the degree of proficiency being practiced in order to invite self-assessment and formative feedback.

Figure 3.1 Rubric for Establishing Shared Vision/Mission, Goals, and Expectations

	Establishing Shared Vision/Mission, Goals, and Expectations		
	Exemplary	**Proficient**	**Progressing**	**Not Meeting Expectations**
Rubric Description	The impact of the leader's actions helps others within the district/ school apply the nine Theories of Practice—powerful behaviors, ways of thinking—to their actions, thereby increasing leadership capacity within the district/school.	The impact of the leader's actions is adequate, necessary, and meets the school needs. Actions relevant to this element are appropriate reflections of quality work with only normal variations.	The impact of the leader's actions reflects performance that shows potential but lacks sufficient proficiencies to improve student learning, instructional practice, and/or other responsibilities.	The impact of the leader's actions demonstrates that the leader either does not understand what is required for proficiency or has demonstrated through his or her action or inaction that he or she chooses not to work toward proficiency.
	In addition to possessing all of the qualities of a "Proficient" leader... The leader routinely shares with others in the district examples of non-judgmental dialogue skills that s/he has used with staff that check and build commitment to goals as well as specific problem-resolving strategies that have contributed to a shared understanding of the current situation, that avoid blame, and that invite a collaborative approach to improvement efforts with colleagues. As a result of sharing these proficient practices with others in the district,	The leader, either directly or through his or her designees, sets, communicates, and monitors a few (two or three) specific schoolwide learning goals, standards, and expectations that have been embedded in school and classroom routines and procedures. The leader develops transparent processes that cause teachers and school leaders to co-create the schoolwide learning goals. The leader also inquires at an early stage about staff capacity to achieve these prioritized goals. Toward that end, the leader goes to exceptional lengths to listen to staff describe their points of view. Furthermore, the	The leader himself or herself sets, communicates, and monitors several (three or four) specific schoolwide learning goals, standards, and expectations. However the goals may not be embedded in school and classroom routines and procedures. The leader sets challenging goals without considering teachers' capacity to achieve them, which causes anxiety to exist among some staff. The leader attempts to involve staff in the goal-setting process, with uneven	The leader himself or herself imposes numerous (more than four) poorly worded, vague learning goals, standards, and expectations. Consequently, these goals, standards, and expectations are not embedded in school and classroom routines and procedures. Because the leader is unaware of teachers' capacity to achieve the goals that s/he has raised, counterproductive levels of anxiety and resentment exist among staff. Moreover, the

(Continued)

51

Figure 3.1 (Continued)

	Establishing Shared Vision/Mission, Goals, and Expectations		
Critical Attributes	there is evidence that by helping others acquire and use the leader's knowledge and skills, they too are achieving at proficient or higher performance levels on this element. **The leader . . .** • Reflects on and secures feedback about the effectiveness of the collaborative problem-solving strategies used to reach agreement among teachers about the importance of the current learning and/or performance goals • Reflects on and secures feedback about the process used to help staff understand the need for, commit to, and believe that they have the capacity to achieve priority goals • Uses and shares with colleagues the information collected through the feedback process to improve others' leadership performance around setting goals, expectations, building commitment, and capacity	leader guarantees the transparent and shared involvement of staff and others in the process so that there is clarity, consensus, and commitment about the goals. **The leader, either directly or through his or her designees . . .** • Engages in collaborative problem solving strategies to reach agreement among teachers about the importance of the current learning and/or performance goals (i.e., by expressing his or her own values and commitments and listening to those of others) • Eliminates stress that may result from multiple conflicting priorities and work overload by focusing on the two or three most important improvement needs • Creates alignment between overarching school goals and the goals set by content area/grade-level leaders • Generates ownership among teachers about the learning goals for which they are responsible by engaging teachers in a co-construction of the overarching school goals	results. Consequently, there may be a lack of clarity, consensus, and commitment to the goals. **The leader, either directly or through his or her designees . . .** • Attempts to engage in collaborative problem-solving strategies but has novice skills in this area, so agreements among teachers as to the importance of the current goals are somewhat mixed, with some agreement and some disagreement • Has begun to prioritize the schools' improvement efforts by focusing on three or four school goals • Understands the importance of having teachers participate in the construction of school goals but has yet to develop an effective process for doing so	leader makes no attempt to involve staff in the goal-setting process. Thus, there is a lack of clarity, consensus, and commitment to the goals. **The leader, either directly or through his or her designees . . .** • Attempts to mitigate conflict and/or gain wider staff commitment by setting far too many goals that lack specificity. In doing so, the leader sends mixed messages about what has priority and what does not • Establishes goals that are imposed rather than co-created collaboratively through discussion with staff • Does not check others commitments to the goals • Is unaware of alignment needs between school and personal goals, which creates a competitive climate

Establishing Shared Vision/Mission, Goals, and Expectations

	• Builds personal commitment among teachers to achieve the goals for which they are responsible • Ensures that teachers have the knowledge and skills that they need to achieve the goals for which they are responsible • Sees to it that teachers have the resources needed to achieve the goals for which they are responsible	• Attempts to create alignment between school goals and personal goals is compromised due to lack of agreement and/or understanding among teachers • Is unable to secure broad (i.e., majority) teacher commitment to goals as they remain uncertain how to reach the goals		• Is unable to secure teacher commitment to the goals as staff members do not understand how what they have differs from what they want
Real-World Examples	*• The leader, when asked, identifies at least one colleague at another school within the district that he or she has personally coached or mentored regarding the goal-setting process.* *• Other leaders in the district credit this leader as a mentor and as a reason for their success in this element.* *• When asked, the leader is able to articulately describe the process that he or she has used to secure feedback as to the effectiveness of the goal- setting process.*	*• A majority of teachers indicate that the leaders in this building invite them into discussions to build a collective rather than imposed set of priority goals.* *• A common refrain from teachers in this building is, "leaders in this building listen to my concerns."* *• A majority of teachers strongly agree or agree with the importance of the current learning goals.* *• When asked, most teachers can articulate how what they have now differs from what they truly want and how this difference represents a need for change.*	*• Teachers generally agree that leaders in this building are beginning to involve them in the goal-setting discussions.* *• When asked, teachers express mixed views as to the importance of current learning goals.* *• Many teachers, when asked, are unable to articulate the reason for current learning goals or the need for change.*	*• When asked, most teachers indicate that the leaders in this building tend to impose goals and expectations without discussion.* *• A majority of teachers strongly disagree or disagree with the importance of the current learning goals.* *• When asked, a majority of teachers express frustration with the multiple conflicting priorities and work overload.*

(Continued)

Figure 3.1   (Continued)

Establishing Shared Vision/Mission, Goals, and Expectations			
• The leader is able to provide evidence of how he or she has used the feedback from the goal-setting process to inform next steps.	• When asked, a majority of teachers say that they are clear about the learning goals for which they are responsible. • A majority of teachers feel personally committed to achieving the goals for which they are responsible. • The leader and/or the leader's designees, when asked, can articulate what they have learned from listening to the concerns of others and how this learning impacted the results of the goal-setting process.	• Teachers express mixed views as to how the goals connect to their day-to-day work. • Fewer than half of the teachers express commitment to the current learning goals.	• Most teachers are unclear about expectations and how the goals connect to them personally. • A majority of teachers lack commitment to achieving the goals.

Element 2: Strategic Resourcing

An integrated and coherent vision of where the organization is heading is the starting point for developing effective strategic resourcing. Strategic resourcing is a key part of strategic human resource management, i.e., matching human resources to the strategic and operational requirements of the organization and ensuring the full utilization of those resources. It is concerned not only with obtaining and keeping the number and quality of staff required but also with selecting and promoting people who "fit" the culture and the strategic requirements of the organization.

The first element of instructional leadership ability concerned the importance of leaders reducing fragmentation and promoting coherence within their school through the process of setting and communicating a few clearly worded goals. The second element, which interacts with the first element, is about leaders taking a "strategic" approach (i.e., a specific pattern of decisions and actions) to how they use money, time, and people such that these resources support the achievement of the school's priority goals. Simply put, the organization's priority goals should drive how leaders organize budgets, schedules, instructional resources, professional development, and staffing. In other words, the leader's goal-related talk must inform the leader's resource-directed walk.

RATIONALE AND DESCRIPTION

Strategic resourcing has an average effect size of 0.31 (Robinson, Lloyd, & Rowe, 2008), suggesting that this type of leadership practice has a small indirect impact on student outcomes. Inasmuch as strategic resourcing sounds simple, it actually requires leaders to manage a great deal of complexity if they are to achieve a tight alignment between priority goals and available resources.

Robinson (2011) suggested that leaders must possess three sets of skills to be successful in practicing this element of instructional leadership ability. To begin with, leaders and/or their designees have to be able to make thoughtful and informed staffing and instructional resource decisions that are more likely to result in goal attainment. Next, effective instructional leadership practice demands that leaders be able to determine the degree to which existing resource-allocation practices are having the desired impact on the school's priority targets. Last, leaders and/or their designees must have strong human relations skills in order to successfully navigate the "human side" (p. 62) of the strategic resource allocation process as they work to reorganize "the people, time, and money in their schools to match their priorities" (Miles & Frank, 2008, p. 11). Moreover, reorganizing how and where these precious resources are to be used requires school leaders and their leadership teams to be courageous as well as persistent in order to generate enough force to break away from the gravitational pull of prior patterns of resourcing that are not producing desired results.

Why must leaders be courageous and persistent? Leaders must be courageous because as they practice the first element of instructional leadership, setting goals and expectations, they establish, both with and through their staff, schoolwide priorities. Consequently, they have to possess determined resolve to say that some things (i.e., instructional practices, curriculum scope and sequence, programs, staffing, etc.) are simply more important than others and then stay the course when champions of those lower priority but favorite programs or practices wish to challenge the decision-making process. Leaders must be persistent because the process of reorganizing or reconstituting resources—including both human resources (i.e., the use of instructional aide positions, instructional specialists, reading coaches, etc.) and the resource of instructional time and how it is used—requires time: time to create a shared vision, time for the vision to take root, and time for the vision to bear fruit. For instance, anyone who has ever attempted to change instructional materials, decide on a new curricular sequence, alter the bell schedule, or implement new instructional practices understands that decisions regarding these resources take time to make and time to deeply implement.

Resourcing Staff Strategically

In his article entitled "Value-Added Assessment from Student Achievement Data: Opportunities and Hurdles," W. L. Sanders (2000) submitted that, "if anyone is serious about improving the academic achievement levels for all students then this improvement will be obtained only be reducing the likelihood that students will be assigned to relatively ineffective teachers" (p. 335). The notion that academic gains for all students will occur by improving instruction has been supported in study after study that has found that one of the most important factors affecting student learning is classroom instruction. Moreover, Saphier, Haley-Speca, and Gower (2008) argued that the quality of teaching (i.e., as perceived by the students, teacher expectations, teachers' conceptions of teaching, learning, assessment, and the students, etc.) dwarf all others in terms of student learning. Consequently, a critical leadership responsibility is for leaders and their leadership teams to improve the quality of teaching within their schools by leveraging their systematic approach to the three "R's" related to staff—Recruitment (including selection), Retention (including support and development [addressed in Element 4]), and Replacement. In brief, leaders and their leadership teams need to have highly refined skills in the area of human capital management.

It is clear that high quality, proactive recruitment and selection of teachers by principals is, at times, constrained by the district's contractual obligations. Regardless, school leaders must work with district policies and officials to "promote a continuum of teacher development that starts with recruitment and continues throughout a teacher's career" (McRobbie, 2000, p. 5) in order to greatly improve teacher quality. Toward that end, we are seeing a growing number of school districts discovering the importance of establishing strong interorganizational partnerships with higher education and teacher-preparation programs that are fueled by the recognition that no one person or organization can fully do the job alone and that each partner has unique needs that will best be met by defining teacher preparation as common work with a shared responsibility. Another way of saying this is that, when leaders weave a web of interconnectivity and collaboration with higher education, they create a powerful web of informed coordinated effort. In this sense, they become webmasters that link people and organizations who do not normally interact with one another.

Moreover, to prepare teachers for 21st century classrooms, teacher education must migrate toward a process in which practitioner knowledge is blended with academic knowledge as prospective teachers learn by doing. In this sense, "school districts can work with preparation program partners to advance new staffing models patterned after teaching hospitals, which will enable clinical faculty, mentors, coaches, teacher interns and residents to work together to better educate students and prospective teachers as part of clinical practice teams" (National Council for Accreditation of Teacher Education, 2010, p. iii).

In addition to districts creating powerful webs of informed coordinated teacher preparation and recruitment partnerships, we have also seen school districts begin to pay more attention to recruiting candidates who they believe are most likely to succeed as teachers. Consequently, they are making use of "smart tools" (Robinson, 2011, p. 69) such as The Gallup Organization's online *TeacherInsight* interview—a 45-minute assessment designed to "identify the best potential teachers" (Gallup Organization, n.d.)—as an additional piece of information to support a district's selection decisions.

In getting new teachers into the classroom, both district leaders and school leaders undertake a series of activities—recruiting qualified applicants, screening them according to evaluative criteria, hiring the most qualified applicants, and placing them where their skills are needed the most. Despite common perceptions, however, effective teachers cannot reliably be identified simply on the basis of information that is typically found in a resume (i.e., where they went to school, their employment experience, their responsibilities, etc.). The best way to assess teachers' effectiveness is to look at their on-the-job performance, including what they do in the classroom and how much progress their students make on achievement tests. This has led to teacher selection processes that allow leaders to actually see teacher candidates in action (i.e., demonstration lessons, videotapes of classroom instruction, use of scenarios, etc.) so that they can more accurately evaluate prospective teachers' on-the-job performance.

For instance, Mary Clement (2008) suggested that the way in which a teacher candidate addressed certain situations in the past yields reliable information as to how the candidate will approach a similar situation in the future. Consequently, she recommended that once interviewers have established the key teaching performance skills that they are looking for in prospective teaching candidates, they apply a practice called "behavior-based interviewing (BBI)" (Clement, 2008, p. 44). The behavior-based interviewing practice requires that interviewers develop "questions that will ascertain whether the candidate has those skills and the experience in applying them" (p. 44). That is, if the interviewer had identified *assessing student learning* as a key performance skill, the interviewer may develop the following interview question: "Describe the various assessments you have found to be most helpful in determining which students are learning and which students need further instruction." Behavior-based interviewing requires interviewers to create questions for each of the key teacher performance skills that go beyond a simple "yes" or "no" response.

While hiring quality teachers is critically important, retaining quality teachers is equally important. According to Richard Ingersoll (2001), Associate Professor within the Graduate School of Education at the University of Pennsylvania, teacher turnover is a particularly troublesome phenomenon that results in staffing problems for school leaders. This revolving-door problem is the result of teachers moving from or leaving their jobs at relatively high rates mostly due to "inadequate support from the school administration, student discipline problems, [and] limited faculty input into school decision-making..." (p. 501). Another way of saying this is that the more support that leaders can provide to new teachers, especially within the first 2–3 years of their employment in these areas, the better. Leaders, through mentoring and well-established organizational socialization processes that help teachers to "learn the ropes" (Louis, 1980), create a sense of obligation and in a sense seduce them to make commitments and feel obligated for the school's support. The result is fewer teachers leaving their teaching assignments.

Earlier, we stated that leaders needed to be courageous and persistent in order to make decisions that best meet student needs. Resourcing staff strategically also requires these same leadership capabilities when it comes to removing staff that consistently demonstrate poor performance. Leaders need courage to confront performance that is potentially harmful to student achievement and persistence to pursue an improvement or termination process. Toward that end, districts have well-established union and district personnel policies and practices that direct school leaders to document performance issues, to clearly convey to the teacher their concerns about performance, and to provide time and opportunities for improvement to occur. However, in the event that support and additional professional development do not raise teacher performance to a satisfactory level, leaders may need to remove the teacher and replace him or her with someone of higher quality. Researchers at the University of Washington (Portin et al., 2009) support the need to at times remove ineffective staff by concluding that sometimes teachers do not work out, acknowledging that while principals hired carefully, they also engaged in the practice of "aggressively weeding out individuals who did not show the capacity to grow" (p. 52).

Resourcing Time Strategically

Unquestionably, recruiting and hiring quality teachers are essential leadership responsibilities. However, this precious human resource will be wasted if instructional time within a school is not also treated as an equally important strategic resource. That is, effective leaders who place a high premium on instructional learning time must make certain that they have an accurate understanding of how instructional time within their classrooms is currently used. The concept of instructional time is defined as the actual time that is genuinely available to teachers for class instruction once such things as announcements, start-of-class and end-of-class transitions, and so on have been removed. Marzano, Kendall, and Gaddy (1999) as well as Miles and Frank (2008) offered a step-by-step guide to this analysis.

Subsequent to leaders making visible how time is distributed within their school, they can proceed to determining whether instructional time should be restructured to allocate more high-quality instruction to students who need it (i.e., scheduling students into two periods of Algebra I, etc.) as well as creating common periods of planning time to their teachers so that they can develop strategies for accelerating the learning of their students. That is, effective leaders work diligently to reverse the typical pattern wherein time is viewed as the constant (i.e., all students take Algebra I for 52 minutes each day) and learning is viewed as the variable (i.e., some students learn Algebra I to high levels within the allocated time and others do not) to make the use of time the variable and learning the constant.

Resourcing Instructional Resources Strategically

The concept of instructional resources includes such things as curriculum guides, textbooks, educational documents that describe curriculum pacing guides and standards, instructional programs (i.e., Piagetian, vocabulary, comprehension, and tactile stimulation programs, etc.), teaching manuals, assessments, and software applications. Consequently, leaders who skillfully work with staff to select these instructional resources understand the magnitude of influence that these decisions have on the success of the organization. Viviane Robinson (2011) underscored the organizational importance of these collective decisions by suggesting that "The influence that school and district leaders exercise through their choice of instructional resources far out-weighs the influence that they exercise through face-to-face interaction because their decisions about which resources to adopt shape the work of so many people" (p. 69).

EVIDENCE OF IMPACT

Leaders demonstrate their knowledge and skills in the area of resourcing strategically by ensuring a tight alignment among key documents (i.e., the school's school-improvement plan, the master schedule, and the annual budget) and processes (i.e., the school's selection and implementation of structured professional learning, hiring of staff, staffing assignments, etc.). Some examples of how leaders can demonstrate evidence of impact in this leadership element follow:

- School leaders routinely evaluate the degree to which the existing allocation of time, staffing, and money are having the desired impact on the school's priority targets.
- School leaders ensure sustained funding for instructional priorities.
- Staff recruitment is based on clear descriptions of teacher effectiveness found within the district's teacher evaluation framework and the students' areas of highest needs.
- School leaders subject the staff recruitment and selection process to an in-depth review and evaluation for the purpose of continuous improvement.
- School leaders can articulate the relationship between instructional programs being implemented and instructional resources being used and student achievement results.
- School leaders know how time is distributed within their school and use this knowledge to make certain that instructional time is

restructured to allocate high-quality instruction to students in the areas of highest need.

- School leaders routinely assess the degree to which relational trust exists among staff in order to successfully navigate the human element of the strategic resource allocation process as they work to reorganize the people, time, and money in their schools to match their priorities.

SUMMARY

Resourcing strategically addresses the issue of school leaders taking a "strategic" approach to how they use money, time, and people such that these resources align with and support the achievement of the school's priority goals. To be successful in practicing this leadership element, leaders must be skilled in three areas. First, they have to be able to make thoughtful and informed staffing and instructional resource decisions that will most likely lead to goal attainment. Second, leaders need to rigorously examine the degree to which existing resource allocation practices are having the desired impact or not on the school's priority targets. Third, leaders must be skilled in the area of human relations as decisions to reorganize how instructional time is used, which instructional practices to take to scale, what instructional materials to adopt and/or abandon, what professional development to pursue, and whether employment of a staff member should be terminated will almost certainly generate a glandular response from staff.

Last, leaders strategically set about improving the academic achievement levels for all students by increasing the likelihood that students will be assigned to effective teachers. The research is clear that the fastest way to improve student achievement is to improve the quality of teachers' instruction. Consequently, leaders must take a proactive approach to recruiting and retaining high-quality teachers by growing their instructional capacity in areas of highest need, and, when necessary, removing ineffective teachers and replacing them with effective teachers.

Figure 4.1 depicts the rubric for Element 2: Strategic Resourcing. The rubric, as with the prior rubrics for previous instructional leadership ability elements, consists of three sections. First, we provide rich "word descriptions" of leadership practice that are situated along a continuum ranging from exemplary on one end to not meeting expectations on the other. Next, we identify the critical attributes of the element; these critical attributes provide essential guidance for observers as well as those being evaluated in distinguishing between practices at adjacent levels of leadership performance. Last, we present possible real-world examples of what the instructional leadership practice looks like according to the degree of proficiency being practiced in order to invite self-assessment and formative feedback.

Figure 4.1 Strategic Resourcing

Strategic Resourcing

	Exemplary	Proficient	Progressing	Not Meeting Expectations
Rubric Description	**In addition to possessing all of the qualities of a "Proficient" leader . . .** The leader provides clear, convincing, and consistent evidence that he or she ensures schoolwide effective use of strategic alignment of resources (human, financial, and material) and individually monitors the impact on student achievement. The leader is skilled in the area of human relations and helps others throughout the district acquire and	The impact of the leader's actions is adequate, necessary, and meets the school needs. Actions relevant to this element are appropriate reflections of quality work with only normal variations.	The impact of the leader's actions reflects performance that shows potential but lacks sufficient proficiencies to improve student learning, instructional practice, and/or other responsibilities.	The impact of the leader's actions demonstrates that the leader either does not understand what is required for proficiency or has demonstrated through his or her action or inaction that he or she chooses not to work toward proficiency.
	The impact of the leader's actions helps others within the district/school apply the nine Theories of Practice—powerful behaviors, ways of thinking—to their actions, thereby increasing leadership capacity within the district/school.	The leader, either directly or through his or her designees, uses the strategic alignment of resources (human, financial, and material) to prioritize and justify the allocation of resources. The leader can determine the type of expertise required to achieve school goals and can legitimately recruit such expertise from within or outside the school. The leader works to develop relationships with the community, higher education, staff developers, and other schools to increase networks of support and resources available to the school. The leader continually evaluates the effectiveness of instructional programs being implemented and instructional resources being used and assesses their impact on student	The leader understands the importance of using strategic alignment of resources (human, financial, and material) to justify the allocation of resources. Because resources have not been prioritized, the leader has diluted his or her efforts to ensure that resources are aligned to school priority needs. The leader inconsistently collects feedback to help determine the effectiveness of instructional programs being implemented and instructional resources being used and their impact on student achievement results. The leader has some	The leader has little or no understanding of the importance of using strategic alignment of resources to prioritize and justify the allocation of resources. Resources are not used to support school priorities, and the leader has not asked for feedback from staff or students regarding the use of resources in the school. The leader has a little or no understanding of the impact of his or her strategic resourcing decisions on staff or students and has not yet

	Strategic Resourcing			
	use these practices so that they too can achieve at the proficient or higher performance levels on this element.	achievement results. The organization's priority goals drive the leader's use of time and how he or she organizes budgets, schedules, instructional resources, professional development, and staffing. The leader demonstrates the ability to "say no" to funding opportunities that overload teachers and detract from priority goals and abandons programs/practices that are not aligned with school goals. The leader is skilled in the area of relational trust and is continually mindful of the impact that his or her strategic resourcing decisions will have on staff.	understanding of the impact of his or her strategic resourcing decisions on staff and has yet to make the needed leadership changes.	decided to, or has decided not to, make the needed leadership changes.
Critical Attributes	**The leader . . .** • Consistently saves resources (time and money) for the organization and proactively redistributes those resources to help the organization achieve its strategic priorities • Continually secures and reflects on feedback from staff and students regarding the allocation of resources to support school priorities and student achievement	**The leader, either directly or through his or her designees . . .** • Routinely evaluates the degree to which the existing allocation of time, staffing, and money is having the desired impact on the school's priority targets • Ensures sustained funding for instructional priorities • Ensures that staff recruitment is based on clear descriptions of teacher effectiveness found within the district's teacher evaluation framework and the students' areas of highest needs • Ensures that the staff recruitment and selection process is subject to an in-depth review and evaluation for continuous improvement purposes	**The leader . . .** • Irregularly evaluates the degree to which the existing allocation of time, staffing, and money is having the desired impact on the school's priority targets • Is beginning to think about a plan for sustaining funding • Has yet to develop a consistent process for the recruitment and hiring of teachers • Implements the districtwide teacher evaluation framework but does not evaluate the effectiveness of teachers' efforts	**The leader . . .** • Has no clear plan for strategically focusing resources on instructional priorities • Has little or no record of monitoring the effectiveness of staff use of instructional time, schedules, teacher evaluation framework, and budgets • Has not secured any additional funding for the school • Is unaware of the degree of relational trust among staff in the school

(Continued)

Figure 4.1 (Continued)

Strategic Resourcing		
• Uses and shares with colleagues the feedback collected and modifications made to their leadership practices so that their practices become as skilled as the leaders' practices • Has established processes to leverage existing limited funds and to increase capacity through grants, donations, and community resourcefulness for the school and district • Is a trusted confidant of district and school leaders and is called upon to share strategic resourcing strategies and systems with other colleagues in order to improve their overall performance	• Articulates the relationship between the instructional programs being implemented and instructional resources being used and the student achievement results being obtained • Knows how time is distributed within the school and uses this knowledge to make certain that instructional time is restructured to allocate high-quality instruction to students in the areas of highest need • Routinely assesses the degree to which relational trust exists among staff in order to successfully navigate the human element of the strategic resources allocation process as he or she works to reorganize the people, time, and money in the schools to match the school's priorities	• Knows the importance of having a relationship between instructional programs being implemented and instructional resources but has yet to articulate the relationship • Has a limited understanding of how instructional time is used throughout the school • Has not formally assessed the degree to which relational trust exists among staff and is not thoroughly aware of the impact of his or her strategic resourcing decisions on staff

Strategic Resourcing

<table>
<tr>
<td rowspan="1">Real-World Examples</td>
<td>

- Results indicate the positive impact of redeployed resources in achieving strategic priorities at the district and school level.
- The leader, when asked, identifies at least one colleague at another school within the district that he or she has personally coached or mentored regarding the strategic resourcing and has evidence to support his or her change in goal-setting process.
- The leader provides documentation reporting that additional dollars from grants and outside sources have been

</td>
<td>

- School financial records reflect alignment of spending with instructional needs.
- Faculty indicates clear protocols for accessing school resources.
- Teachers self-report that the school recruiting and interview processes are fair and transparent.
- School Improvement Plan and budget expenditures are directly aligned.
- Leader's documents reveal recurring involvement in aligning time, facility use, and human resources with priority school needs.
- Schedules and calendars reflect attention to instructional priorities.
- Schoolwide teacher questionnaire results reveal satisfaction with resources provided for instructional and faculty development.
- Students acknowledge that an adequate amount of instructional time is available to them in areas of highest need.
- Teachers can describe the process for accessing and spending money in support of instructional priorities.

</td>
<td>

- Teachers generally agree that the leader involves them in decisions regarding the use of school resources and that the use of these resources is beginning to have a greater alignment with school priorities.
- Many teachers, when asked, are unable to articulate a consistent process for the hiring of teachers at the school.
- The budget reflects that the leader has made minimal attempts to secure added resources.
- The budget reflects inconsistent use in focusing resources on school improvement priorities.
- Less than half of the staff schedules and calendars reflect attention to instructional priorities.
- Fewer than half of the students, when asked, state.

</td>
<td>

- Teachers self-report that they feel overloaded and are detracted from priority goals due to ineffective use of resources.
- Most teachers, when asked, report that they are not aware of the hiring practices used at the school.
- Office budget documents reflect that dollars are not committed or used until late in the year or are carried over to another year due to lack of planning and coordination and that there is no focus on resources used on school improvement priorities.
- Schedules and calendars do not reflect attention to instructional priorities.
- The budget shows no attempt to secure outside resources.

</td>
</tr>
</table>

(Continued)

Figure 4.1 (Continued)

Strategic Resourcing		
utilized to support school priorities. • When asked, the leader can articulate and provide evidence of the process that he or she used to secure feedback form staff and students as to the effective school use of their strategic resources • Students self-report that they have all of the resources needed at the school to successfully accomplish their learning goals.	• The leader and/or the leader's designee, when asked, can articulate what he or she has learned from securing staff feedback and can share leadership changes that have been made as a result of the feedback.	that they have the resources needed to support their learning goals at school.

Element 3:
Ensuring
Teacher and
Staff
Effectiveness

F ew topics in education have captured as much attention from policy makers and practitioners as the connection between teaching quality and student achievement. The research has clearly shown that quality teaching matters to student learning. Teacher quality has been consistently identified as the most important school-based factor in student achievement.

Toward that end, highly effective principals relentlessly work to improve student achievement by ensuring teacher and staff effectiveness. They help to define and promote clear goals and high expectations, they strive to reduce teacher isolation and fragmented effort, and they establish direct linkages with teachers and between teachers and the classroom (Portin et al., 2009). Effective principals understand that what makes the difference is not a particular strategy; rather, it is ensuring that teachers' professional learning centers on such things as "when to provide different or more effective strategies for teaching and learning" (Hattie, 2009, p. 245) and initiating discussions about instructional approaches, both in teams and with individual teachers. Moreover, they pursue these key leadership strategies despite the common refrain that we hear from so many teachers with whom we interact to simply "leave me alone and let me teach."

RATIONALE AND DESCRIPTION

Robinson, Lloyd, and Rowe's (2008) meta-analysis revealed that this leadership dimension (our third element of instructional leadership ability), similar to the first element, has a moderate impact on student achievement outcomes (effect size [ES], 0.42). In his discussion on the topic of effect size and degree of impact, Hattie (2009) instructively pointed out that an effect size of ≥0.40 establishes a benchmark at which real-world change occurs. This particular leadership practice eclipses that threshold.

So, in what actions do leaders of high-performing schools engage if they are ensuring teacher and staff effectiveness? Essentially, leadership accomplishes this task by engaging in four sets of interdependent practices, sub-elements, if you will, to this third element within our framework. First, the research suggests that schools that are able to demonstrate increased coherence of curriculum, instruction, and assessment also show marked improvements in student performance. Leaders of schools that have a coherent instructional program have worked with their teachers to link their curriculum to stated learning goals and use common instructional strategies with fidelity. Teachers coordinate curriculum and assessments to avoid repetition and to offer students new and more complex aspects of subject matter from grade to grade. School-sponsored support programs, such as instructional interventions, assemblies, field trips, tutoring, and parent education, are linked to curriculum, instruction, and assessment. Leaders, along with the leadership team, strategically accept and reject programs and initiatives that do not support the school's focus, program continuity, and ongoing improvement (Newmann, Smith, Allensworth, & Bryk, 2001).

Second, leaders engage in ongoing dialogue with faculty about the relationship of teaching and leadership practices to student achievement. For example, highly effective leaders are guided by such questions as, "What do we know about our impact on all students?" and "How do we know it?" and "To what extent do data and evidence drive practice in our school?" Toward that end, leaders and teachers together, among other things, track student progress by calculating effect sizes on cohorts of students from one year to the next in order to determine whether students are growing by at least a year for a year's worth of instruction. Leaders in academically growing schools help teachers know how to calculate and use effect sizes within their classrooms so they can look at total effect size gains for the class as a whole as well as for individual students. Last, leaders calculate and use teacher-by-teacher effect size data to determine which teachers were most effective and which were least effective, not to rate or berate teachers, but rather to determine the specific practices of the most effective teachers so that these practices can be replicated by their peers throughout the school.

Ongoing dialogue between teachers and leaders about student achievement growth, however, does not just happen. It is clear from the research that school leaders in higher performing schools distinguish themselves from their peers in lower performing schools by creating structures and opportunities that allow teachers to engage in continuous and sustained learning about their practices in the setting in which they actually work. Moreover, highly skilled leaders help their teacher colleagues examine how well students are doing by calculating teacher-by-teacher and student-by-student effect size data, developing a convergence of meaning by making critical sense of it, and then relating this information to how they are teaching in order to make continuous improvements. Robinson (2011) referred to this type of ongoing dialogue as "linking talk" (p. 110) whereby school and teacher leaders steer teachers to link their discussions of student learning to the environment they have established within the classroom and to their own instructional practices.

Third, the frequent presence of leaders within classrooms for the purpose of observing the impact of teachers' work on student learning and providing them with subsequent feedback is a hallmark of leaders in higher performing schools. Wahlstrom, Louis, Leithwood, and Anderson (2010) echoed this sentiment in the findings from their study by stating,

> High-scoring principals frequently observed classroom instruction for short periods of time, making 20-60 observations a week, and most of the observations were spontaneous. Their visits enabled them to make formative observations that were clearly about learning and professional growth, coupled with direct and immediate feedback. (p. 86)

In a related manner, highly effective leaders tend to keep track of teachers' professional development needs that are focused on the common instructional framework. For example, subsequent to teachers' introduction to a new instructional strategy, teachers are provided with several opportunities to critically examine it, to implement it within their classrooms, to self-assess themselves, and to receive feedback from leaders, colleagues, and outside experts against the established learning intentions and success criteria. Furthermore, the new instructional strategy becomes a focus for teacher discussion and reflection for an extended period of time (several months or even years).

Fourth, the methodical monitoring and use of student performance data to drive continuous program improvement is essential for ensuring quality teaching. Why? Because student achievement results, whether they are what we hope to see or want desperately to avoid, do not just happen! They have antecedents. That is, just as we discovered in the second leadership practice leading to quality teaching, there is a relationship between specific strategies in teaching, leadership, and curriculum and student achievement results. Consequently, leaders must have a clear understanding with regard to which programs and practices are not having the desired kind of impact on student achievement so they can move quickly to either modify or eliminate them and also with regard to which programs and practices are having a positive impact on student achievement so they can take them to scale within the organization.

EVIDENCE OF IMPACT

Information showing leaders' skill at enhancing the quality of teaching within their school is primarily derived from four sources. First, the leaders' skill at improving the quality of teaching in classrooms happens based on the examination and use of information derived from face-to-face interviews and/or surveys that focus on both the frequency and quality of dialogue occurring between teachers, leaders, and leadership teams. Second, the leader's skill in the area of enhancing quality teaching results from the examination of key curriculum, instruction, and assessment documents (i.e., curriculum guides, pacing guides, teacher-made assessments, summaries of program evaluation, etc.). Third, leaders and teachers both routinely calculate and use effect size data to determine the growth in student learning that is or is not occurring. Fourth, leaders and teachers learn about the quality of teaching by tapping into student perspectives as to what learning looks and feels like. Some examples of how leaders can demonstrate evidence of impact in this element of instructional leadership ability include

- A clear understanding among teachers as to which high-priority academic standards are orchestrated horizontally within and vertically across all grade levels
- Agreement among teachers that the teaching of high-priority academic standards is driven by the use of a common instructional framework
- The proportion of teacher assessments that measure the things that teachers really value
- The level of agreement that exists between teachers and the leadership team about what constitutes effective teaching and learning
- The degree to which student evaluations of teachers are used as an index of teaching quality
- The percentage of teachers whose yearly effect size measures are ≥ 0.40
- The degree of understanding among the staff as to which instructional and leadership strategies and curricular programs are having the greatest impact on student achievement and which are not, which informs next steps

- The frequency and quality of "linking talks" (i.e., connecting teaching to student learning) that occur among teachers and leaders within the school
- The frequency with which leaders are present within classrooms in order to observe the impact of teachers' work on student learning and provide them with subsequent feedback
- The degree to which student achievement data are regularly monitored and used to determine program effectiveness

SUMMARY

In summary, leaders of higher performing schools work directly with and tirelessly for teachers to plan, orchestrate, and evaluate teachers, leaders, and leading. Four sets of interdependent leadership practices that ensure the quality of teaching were identified. First, the orchestration of a coherent instructional program is a byproduct of a leader's skill at working with his or her teachers to link the curriculum to stated learning goals, using common instructional strategies with fidelity, and coordinating curriculum and assessments from grade to grade. Leaders ensure that school-sponsored support programs are coupled to curriculum, instruction, and assessment within and across grades and, along with the leadership team, strategically accept and reject programs and initiatives that do not support the school's focus, program continuity, and ongoing improvement. Second, leaders help teachers examine how well students are doing, relate this information to how well they are teaching, and then make improvements based on those critical, ongoing "linking talks" (Robinson, 2011, p. 110). Third, leaders have an acute awareness of teaching and learning needs in their schools because of their frequent presence within classrooms. Fourth, leaders of high-performing schools have a systematic process for monitoring and then using student perception and performance data to inform continuous program improvement.

Figure 5.1 depicts the rubric for Element 3: "Ensuring Teacher and Staff Effectiveness." The rubric, as with the rubrics for the previous elements of instructional leadership ability, consists of three sections. First, we provide rich "word descriptions" of leadership practice that are situated along a continuum ranging from exemplary on one end to not meeting expectations on the other. Next, we identify the critical attributes of the element; these critical attributes provide essential guidance for observers as well as those being evaluated in distinguishing between practices at adjacent levels of leadership performance. Last, we present possible real-world examples of what the instructional leadership practice looks like according to the degree of proficiency being practiced in order to invite self-assessment and formative feedback.

Figure 5.1 Rubric for Ensuring Teacher and Staff Effectiveness

Ensuring Teacher and Staff Effectiveness

	Exemplary	Proficient	Progressing	Not Meeting Expectations
Rubric Description	The impact of the leader's actions helps others within the district/school apply the nine Theories of Practice—powerful behaviors, ways of thinking—to their actions, thereby increasing leadership capacity within the district/school.	The impact of the leader's actions is adequate, necessary, and meets the school needs. Actions relevant to this element are appropriate reflections of quality work, with only normal variations.	The impact of the leader's actions reflects performance that shows potential but lacks sufficient proficiencies to improve student learning, instructional practice, and/or other responsibilities.	The impact of the leader's actions demonstrates that the leader either does not understand what is required for proficiency or has demonstrated through his or her action or inaction that he or she chooses not to work toward proficiency.
	In addition to possessing all of the qualities of a "Proficient" leader . . . The leader provides clear, convincing, and consistent evidence that he or she builds the capacity of staff to effectively develop, adapt, and implement a rigorous curriculum; implements a variety of rigorous instructional strategies and pedagogical methods; adapts instruction and assessment; and uses multiple sources of disaggregated quantitative and qualitative	The leader, either directly or through his or her designees, works with and tirelessly for teachers to plan, orchestrate, and evaluate teachers, leaders, and leading. The leader engages in four sets of interdependent leadership practices to ensure the quality of teaching: • First, the leader orchestrates a coherent instructional program, which is a byproduct of his or her skill at working with teachers to link the curriculum to stated learning goals. The leader uses common instructional strategies with fidelity and coordinates the	The leader works directly with teachers to plan, orchestrate, and evaluate teachers. However, his or her engagement in key leadership practices to ensure the quality of teaching is haphazard. Consequently: • A plan for the development of a coherent instructional program may not yet be fully implemented. The leader understands the importance of using common instructional strategies but either does not know where to start or tries to focus on	The leader does not know and/or chooses not to interact with staff about planning, orchestrating, and evaluating teachers. Therefore: • The leader is unaware of curriculum needs because he or she has little or no interaction with staff concerning assessment and knowledge and/or skills of assessment literacy and data analysis. • The leader chooses not to interact with staff

data to address student learning needs that will close achievement gaps. Moreover, the leader helps others throughout the district acquire and use these practices so that they too can achieve at the proficient or higher performance levels on this particular element.

curriculum and assessments from grade to grade. The leader ensures that school-sponsored support programs are linked to curriculum, instruction, and assessment within and across grades. The leader, along with the leadership team, strategically accepts and rejects programs and initiatives that do not support the school's focus, program continuity, and ongoing improvement.

- Second, the leader helps teachers examine together how well students are doing, link this information to how well they are teaching (i.e., calculating effect size by cohorts, teachers, and students), and then make improvements based on those critical, ongoing "linking talks."
- Third, the leader has an acute awareness of teaching and learning needs in the school because of his or her frequent presence within classrooms with subsequent feedback to teachers.
- Fourth, the leader has a systematic process for monitoring and then using student performance data to inform continuous program improvement.

too many strategies at one time. Coordination of the curriculum and assessments from grade to grade is occurring, but in a limited number of areas.

- The leader, together with teachers, examines how well students are doing; however, the teachers may not be linking this information to how well they are teaching.
- The leader understands the importance of frequent classroom observations, but it occurs infrequently and may not always include feedback.
- The absence of a systematic process for monitoring and then using student performance data complicates improvement efforts.

about the use of research-based instructional strategies to increase student achievement to high levels for all students.

- The leader focuses primarily on the managerial functions of the role, which tend to trump classroom observations; thus, the leader's presence in classrooms occurs infrequently, with little to no feedback to teachers.
- The leader is indifferent to data and does not use data to change schedules, instruction, curriculum, or leadership practices.

(Continued)

Figure 5.1 (Continued)

Ensuring Teacher and Staff Effectiveness

Critical Attributes		
The leader . . . • Builds the capacity of faculty to effectively develop, adapt, and implement rigorous Common Core State Standards to effectively address all student learning needs • Builds the capacity of staff to effectively implement a variety of rigorous strategies and pedagogical methods (ES ≥0.40) that help students exceed expectations • Helps faculty adapt instruction and assessments to ensure that all students master content and demonstrate at least a year's growth (ES ≥0.40) for a year's worth of instruction • Uses multiple sources of quantitative data (e.g., percentage of students achieving proficiently or higher on local assessments,	**The leader, either directly or through his or her designees...** • Establishes with teachers clarity as to which high-priority Common Core State Standards are orchestrated horizontally within and vertically across all grade levels • Determines with teachers that the teaching of high-priority Common Core State Standards is driven by the use of a common instructional framework • Confirms with teachers a close relationship between the things that teachers really value and the teacher-made assessments that are used • Achieves a high level of agreement with teachers as to what constitutes effective teaching and learning • Agrees to use student evaluations of teachers as an index of teaching quality, the results of which drive instructional improvement	**The leader . . .** • Is aware of the need for high-priority Common Core State Standards; however, the school is still in the planning stages of developing its priority standards • Has yet to identify and implement a common instructional framework • Has yet to analyze the degree to which teacher-made assessments align with important teacher needs • Is aware of what effective teaching and learning looks like; however, agreement with teachers on these matters is not yet evident • Does not understand the research on student evaluations of teachers as an index of teaching quality • Is not certain which instructional and leadership strategies and curricular programs are having the	**The leader . . .** • Does not know and/or is uninterested in the need to identify high-priority academic standards • Leaves the matter of an instructional framework up to individual teachers to determine • Determines what effective teaching and learning look like, and these views are reflected in teacher evaluations • Is unaware of which instructional and leadership strategies and curricular programs are having the greatest impact on student achievement • Believes that the qualities that students bring with them to school are largely unchangeable by his or her teachers • Is present in classrooms fewer than 10 times

Ensuring Teacher and Staff Effectiveness

			per month to observe teachers' work, with suggestions and advice offered but not feedback being provided to teachers • Rarely monitors and uses student achievement data to determine program effectiveness
		greatest impact on student achievement • Understands the need to have teachers engage in dialogue about the relationship of teaching practices to student achievement, but this practice is not schoolwide • Is present in classrooms 10 to 20 times per month in order to observe teachers' work and provides suggestions and/or praise to teachers at times about their practice not about the impact of their practice on student learning • Inconsistently monitors and uses student achievement data to determine program effectiveness	
percentage of faculty implementing the current professional development training at the proficient or higher levels) and qualitative data (e.g., video diaries, focus groups, interviews) to assess and monitor learning; creates systems for consistent monitoring and frequent (i.e., monthly) collection of data; and uses data appropriately to identify student achievement trends and patterns, prioritize needs, and drive improvement efforts	• Systematically measures the percentage of teachers whose yearly effect size (ES) is ≥0.40 as a measure of teacher effectiveness • Ascertains a high degree of understanding among the staff as to which instructional and leadership strategies and curricular programs are having the greatest impact on student achievement and which are not in order to inform next steps • Establishes a routine of frequent (i.e., monthly) "linking talks" with and among teachers and leaders within the school to help them make critical sense of their teaching and student learning • Is present in classrooms 20 to 60 times per week to observe the impact of teachers' work on student learning and provide and secures from them feedback • Systematically and regularly monitors and uses student achievement and perception data to determine program effectiveness		

(Continued)

Figure 5.1 (Continued)

Ensuring Teacher and Staff Effectiveness			
Real-World Examples	• "Our principal ensures that all students get high quality teachers." • The leader, when asked, identifies at least one colleague at another school within the district that he or she had personally coached or mentored regarding his or her knowledge and skills in ensuring teacher effectiveness. • Other leaders in the district credit this leader as a mentor and a reason for their success in developing and implementing effective feedback systems. • "When teachers are struggling, my principal provides support for them." • Other leaders in the district credit this leader as a mentor and a reason for their success in.	• "My school administrator leads formal discussions concerning instruction and student achievement." • Understands and uses student data to collaboratively diagnose and resolve teaching problems and to set future goals • "My school administrator has a research-based understanding of how students learn." • "My school administrator uses clearly communicated criteria for judging my performance." • "My school administrator makes frequent, at least monthly, classroom observations and provides feedback regarding the impact of my instruction on student learning." • "My school administrator's appraisal of my teaching performance helps me improve my performance."	• "My principal promotes discussion of instructional issues." • Understands and uses student data to diagnose and resolve teaching problems and to set future goals. • "My principal's understanding of how students learn is based on her personal experience." • "My principal uses the district teacher evaluation criteria for judging my performance." • "My principal makes 3 or 4 classroom observations per year and provides advice or praise regarding my instruction." • "My principal's appraisal of my teaching performance validates for me what I know I do well!"	• "My principal believes teachers discuss instructional issues when they meet in their content area teams." • Uses student data to highlight success in or problems with teaching. • Student learning is viewed largely as a byproduct of their demographics. • "My principal makes 1 or 2 classroom observations per year and provides advice or suggestions or praise regarding my instruction." • "My principal's appraisal of my teaching performance is a compliance task."

Ensuring Teacher and Staff Effectiveness

using multiple sources of quantitative data (e.g., percentage of students achieving proficiently or higher on local assessments, percentage of faculty implementing the current professional development training at the proficient or higher levels) and qualitative data (e.g., video diaries, focus groups, interviews) to assess and monitor learning.	• *"My school administrator is accessible to discuss matters dealing with instruction."* • Establishes clear data analysis procedures that ensure faculty will regularly use evidence to review student progress. • *"My school administrator assists faculty in calculating effect size and interpreting test results."* • *"My school administrator clearly defines school wide standards for instructional practices."*	• *"My principal encourages me to discuss matters dealing with instruction with my grade-level leader."* • Directs faculty to use evidence from the state assessment to determine student progress	• *"My principal assumes that if I need to discuss instructional matters, I would do so with my content area teams."* • Uses student data as a lever to demand better instructional performance

Element 4:
Leading and
Participating
in Teacher/
Leader Learning
and Development

U nlike the previous three elements, the fourth element, *Leading and Participating in Teacher/Leader Learning and Development,* has, on average, a large and educationally significant impact (Robinson, Lloyd, & Rowe, 2008) on student achievement with an effect size of 0.84. The magnitude of this effect "provides some empirical support for calls to school leaders to be actively involved with their teachers as the 'leading learners' of their school" (p. 663). Karen Seashore-Louis, Professor of Educational Policy and Administration at the University of Minnesota, and Kenneth Leithwood, Professor of Educational Leadership and Policy at Ontario Institute for Studies in Education at the University of Toronto (Louis et al., 2010), lead a team of researchers who echo the findings of Robinson, Lloyd, and Rowe. Specifically, these researchers concluded that, among other things, principals play a key role in supporting and encouraging teachers' professional growth. Moreover, the researchers discovered that high-scoring principals in their study were characterized as "having a hands-on, direct role in instructional operations" (p. 87). Leading teacher learning and development is clearly one of the most impactful of leadership strategies in which school leaders should be engaged.

RATIONALE AND DESCRIPTION

Research plainly supports the fact that sustained and intensive professional learning for teachers is related to student achievement gains. That is the good news! The bad news is that for professional learning to be effective it must be intensive, ongoing, and connected to practice; it must focus on the teaching and learning of specific academic content; it must be connected to other school initiatives; and it must build strong working relationships among teachers. So what is the problem? Most teachers across most states, districts, and schools in the United States do not have access to professional learning opportunities that uniformly meet all of these criteria (Darling-Hammond, Wei, Andree, Richardson, & Orphanos, 2009).

The problem of lack of access to quality professional learning opportunities is followed by yet a second problem. The second problem is that this element of instructional leadership ability is described as *Leading and Participating in Teacher/Leader Learning and Development*. The operative word is *leading* as this element involves more than simply having leaders arrange for and orchestrate teachers' professional learning opportunities. In other words, while it is important for leaders to make thoughtful and informed decisions about the type of professional development that promotes goal achievement (Element 2), supporting and resourcing professional learning is, by itself, insufficient. Leaders must serve in dual roles as both leaders of, and participants within, the scheduled teacher professional learning. In so doing, principals help teachers translate learning into practice. This kind of purposeful collaboration reinforces the school's focus, builds coherence in otherwise fragmented systems, and underpins the idea that working together toward a common purpose is a valuable enterprise because of its contribution to building trust, collective responsibility, and a schoolwide focus on learning for all.

What then might be some of the key reasons as to why this leadership element is so impactful? The first possibility is that leaders' endorsement of and involvement in teacher professional learning is visible evidence of their desire to impact the quality of teachers and teaching (Element 3). Earlier, we suggested that teacher quality has been consistently identified as the most important school-based factor in student achievement. Consequently, in order for leaders to have such a focus, it is reasonable to assume that, as leaders engage with teachers in purposeful collaboration about their learning and development, student achievement will be positively impacted. This certainly was reflected in the findings of the research by Louis et al. (2010), who described high-scoring principals within their study as being "actively engaged in providing direct instructional support to teachers" (p. 85). Teachers working with high-scoring principals tended to view their principal as instructional leaders, with both the teachers and the principals getting and giving feedback about the quality of the instruction

A second possibility is that as leaders join with teachers in a partnership approach to improved teaching practices, they come to learn about the challenges that teachers face and how best to provide support. Principals, for example, can create opportunities to learn *along* with teachers by having one-on-one conversations during which they ask teachers about relevant classroom experiences or by sitting down with groups of teachers to examine the quality of student work vis-à-vis specific instructional standards, together making the link to particular instructional practices, tracking the progress of each and every student, and identifying changes in practice that have a high probability of resulting in increased student learning. More importantly, for these principals, each day offers a new opportunity for learning, and, when principals come to teachers with a genuine desire to hear and learn from them, they demonstrate a deep regard for the professionals within their school. Next, we describe several factors that, according to research, have been shown to promote professional learning; these factors include the context in which professional learning occurs, the qualities of the content that is used to achieve the professional learning, the specific activities that advance professional learning, and the attributes of the learning process that are associated with effective professional learning.

With regard to the context within which effective professional learning occurs, the research by Timperley, Wilson, Barrar, & Fung (2007) suggested that leaders should pay attention to seven factors that appear to be hallmarks of effective professional development:

- Successful professional interventions are guided by explicit professional learning goals that are linked to student outcomes.
- The content that is presented during the professional learning time is of high quality.
- Outside expertise (i.e., someone outside the school or a high-status person from within the school) is employed to challenge the status quo.
- Leaders participate in the professional learning even if they lack relevant expertise.
- The professional learning shifts the discourse from blaming students and parents to teachers accepting more responsibility on how to teach the most academically challenged groups of students within their school.
- Learning new ideas and practices takes time (i.e., six months to five years), with massive amounts of initial input followed by spaced opportunities to learn.

- The professional learning challenges existing assumptions yet at the same time provides alternative instructional theories designed to better meet the needs of students.

With regard to the content that is used to achieve professional learning, the researchers identified several qualities that were most closely associated with a larger impact on student achievement. Specifically, the most effective content linked theoretical principles with practical examples, used specific problems in the teacher-student relationships as a motivator for teachers to participate, created a vision of teaching and learning galvanized with practical examples and evidence of the potential impact on student achievement, and created an understanding that changes in instructional methods trigger changes in teacher-student relationships whereby it is necessary for teachers and students to co-construct the meaning of the content being taught.

With regard to the types of activities that are most likely to advance professional learning, the researchers identified four qualities: (1) professional instruction accompanied by theoretical overviews that challenge existing assumptions followed by multiple opportunities for teachers to learn, (2) opportunities for teachers to practice new learning and uncover problems related to implementation, (3) opportunities for teachers to compare the relationship of their practice to teacher-student relationships and student understanding, and (4) galvanized participation in professional learning communities, which offers opportunities for teachers to plan and make sense of the new knowledge and skills.

Last, the research revealed important attributes of the learning processes associated with effective professional learning. To begin with, changes in teacher practices occurred when the professional learning challenged the teachers' existing assumptions about relationships, instructional methods, and student achievement. Next, the professional learning created opportunities for teachers to learn and to change their practice as new information was presented and as teachers' understanding was expanded. Then, when teachers were forced to wrestle with new pedagogy and develop self-regulatory skills (i.e., setting goals for students, teacher self-monitoring, self-assessing, self-evaluation, and providing self-feedback) their practice changed. Consequently, leaders of quality professional learning play a key role in fostering teachers' success. Effective leaders of professional development are highly skilled in facilitating teacher learning.

EVIDENCE OF IMPACT

Leaders demonstrate their evolving knowledge and skill in the area of leading high-quality, collaborative, teacher and leader learning and development by providing evidence that they are applying the research on professional learning that shifts teachers practices and enhances student learning. Some examples of how leaders can demonstrate evidence of impact in this instructional leadership ability element follow:

- The characteristics of effective professional learning, as described within the research, drive the design, selection, and implementation of teacher and leader professional learning opportunities.
- Teachers agree that leaders in their school routinely participate with them as the leader, learner, or at times both during professional learning opportunities.
- Teachers agree that, as a group and as subgroups, they examine together how well students are doing, relate this information to how they are teaching, and then make the necessary adjustments in pedagogy.
- There are clear connections between the planned professional development and students' learning needs.
- Both teachers' and leaders' deliberate practice plans (i.e., personal improvement plans) are directly linked to student learning needs.
- The leader can articulate the system that he or she uses to identify teachers with the expertise that is needed to help colleagues address targeted teaching problems.
- Teachers and leaders agree that they routinely measure the degree to which student learning has been impacted as a result of changes in pedagogy resulting from professional learning.

SUMMARY

When it comes to impacting student achievement, the most powerful leadership practices are those contained within the fourth element: *Leading and Participating in Teacher/Leader Learning and Development*. These practices require the leader to first and foremost be a leader of, and at the same time be a participant within, teachers' professional learning experiences. Furthermore, we established that leaders must identify, resource, and implement high-quality collaborative opportunities for teachers to improve their specific knowledge and skills sets in order to help all students move with success and confidence to the next educational level. The research on the aspects of professional development that promote teacher learning in ways that result in changed pedagogical methods and advancements in student learning provides leaders with good guidance. These aspects include specifically focusing on both student and teacher learning needs, emphasizing the importance of relationship between instructional/leadership practice and student achievement, offering teachers valuable content that integrates both theory and practice, employing the services of external expertise, and providing time for teachers to have multiple opportunities to practice, receive feedback, and receive ongoing support as they work to implement new learning.

Figure 6.1 depicts the rubric for Element 4. The rubric, as with the rubrics for previous instructional leadership ability elements, consists of three sections. First, we provide rich "word descriptions" of leadership practice that are situated along a continuum ranging from exemplary on one end to not meeting expectations on the other. Next, we identify the critical attributes of the element; these critical attributes provide essential guidance for observers as well as those being evaluated in distinguishing between practices at adjacent levels of leadership performance. Last, we present possible real-world examples of what the instructional leadership practice looks like according to the degree of proficiency being practiced in order to invite self-assessment and formative feedback.

Figure 6.1   Rubric for Leading and Participating in Teacher/Leader Learning and Development

	Leading and Participating in Teacher/Leader Learning and Development		
	Exemplary	**Proficient**	**Progressing**	**Not Meeting Expectations**
Rubric Description	The impact of the leader's actions help others within the district/school apply the nine Theories of Practice—powerful behaviors, ways of thinking—to their actions, thereby increasing leadership capacity within the district/school. **In addition to possessing all of the qualities of a "Proficient" leader . . .** The leader has clearly demonstrated a record of differentiated job-embedded professional learning focused on the implementation of instructional priorities and faculty and student needs. Teachers and leaders routinely share instructional practices, and teachers in the building as well as school leaders are asked to share their expertise and experiences within the school as well as with other schools in the district to improve	The impact of leader's actions is adequate, necessary, and meets the school needs. Actions relevant to this element are appropriate reflections of quality work, with only normal variations. The leader, either directly or through his or her designees, impacts student achievement by leading and participating in professional learning experiences with staff. The leader applies the professional learning research that shifts teachers' practices and promotes the learning of students. The leader identifies, resources, and implements high-quality collaborative opportunities for teachers, promoting teacher learning in ways that result in changed pedagogical methods and advancements in student learning. Learning includes a specific focus on both student and teacher/leader learning needs, emphasizing the importance	The impact of the leader's actions reflects performance that shows potential but lacks sufficient proficiencies to improve student learning, instructional practice, and/or other responsibilities. The leader attempts to implement professional learning experiences but has not yet connected these experiences to the school plan, to the research, and to priority instructional needs and has not made time to be part of the training. Time for professional learning is provided but is not a consistent priority and usually takes place during faculty meetings. There is limited evidence of job-embedded professional learning, and teachers have little ownership of advocating for and	The impact of the leader's actions demonstrate that he or she either does not understand what is required for proficiency or has demonstrated through his or her action or inaction that he or she chooses not to work toward proficiency. The leader provides and/ or supports large group unfocused professional learning that reflects little or no evidence of acknowledgment of individual faculty needs or alignment of faculty needs to student achievement needs. Professional learning practices at the school are not monitored and are not necessarily aligned to the school priorities. Staff feel fragmented and unfocused and do not know where to turn for instructional support.

Figure 6.1 (Continued)

Leading and Participating in Teacher/Leader Learning and Development

Critical Attributes		

the practices of others. Teachers along with school leaders see themselves as learners and have established a high degree of relational trust. School achievement improvement data reflect the leader's and teachers' focus on specific professional learning goals.

of relationship between instructional/leadership practice and student achievement, offering teachers valuable content that integrates both theory and practice, employing the services of external expertise, and providing teachers with time to have multiple opportunities to practice, to receive feedback (i.e., six months to five years), and to receive ongoing support as they work to implement new learning. The leader engages in strategic planning whereby both leaders and teachers share leadership practices, which strengthens the professional community, resulting in stronger working relationships and higher student achievement.

determining their needs. It is not clear if there is a connection between student achievement and professional development at the school.

The leader . . .

- Is well versed in the effective professional learning research and has clear, convincing, documented evidence showing the degree to which student learning has been impacted

The leader, either directly or through his or her designees . . .

- Ensures that effective professional learning, as described within the research, drives the design, selection, and implementation of teacher professional learning opportunities

The leader . . .

- Attempts to use effective professional learning, as described within the research, to drive the design, selection, and implementation of teacher professional learning

The leader . . .

- Is not aware of the effective professional development research; therefore, he or she randomly designs professional learning opportunities for teachers with no attention to

Leading and Participating in Teacher/Leader Learning and Development			
as a result of changes in pedagogy resulting from professional learning. As a result, the leader has been asked by district and/or school colleagues to be a coach and/or mentor to others within the district. • Is actively involved as a leader and learner during professional learning opportunities at both the school and district levels • Ensures that teachers' and leaders' deliberate practice plans (i.e., professional growth plans) are linked to student learning needs and has helped teachers and other school leaders understand the relationship between student learning and their teaching by helping others track and share the student achievement and adult data within their school at monthly planning meetings. The leader has also helped other school leaders in writing, implementing and monitoring of their deliberate practice plans.	• Routinely participates with teachers as the leader, learner, or both during professional learning opportunities • Ensures that teachers, both as a group and as subgroups, examine together how well students are doing, relate this information to how they are teaching, and then make the necessary adjustments in pedagogy • Articulates clear connections between the planned professional development and students' learning needs • Ensures that teachers' and leaders' deliberate practice plans (i.e., professional growth plans) are linked to student learning needs • Articulates the system that he or she uses to identify teachers with the expertise that is needed to help colleagues address targeted teaching problems • Routinely measures the degree to which student learning has been impacted as a result of changes in pedagogy resulting from professional learning	opportunities but has yet to develop a cohesive plan • Inconsistently participates with teachers as the leader, learner, or both during professional learning opportunities • Has set up planning time for teachers to meet together to examine how well students are doing but has not helped teachers to see the relationship between student achievement and their teaching in order to make the necessary adjustments in pedagogy • Has yet to develop clear connections between the planned professional development and students' learning needs • Ensures that leaders' deliberate practice plans (i.e., professional growth plans) are linked to student learning needs but has yet to link teachers' plans to student achievement	monitoring the effectiveness of the professional development • Is absent from professional learning opportunities for teachers or leaders • Leader and teacher professional growth plans co not align with high priority student achievement needs • Uses only the assigned building coach or other assistant principals to mentor teachers • Provides minimal opportunities for faculty to engage in collegial professional development processes in the school

(Continued)

Figure 6.1 (Continued)

Leading and Participating in Teacher/Leader Learning and Development			
• Has developed and implemented a comprehensive teacher support plan after evaluating all staff needs, strengths, and areas of expertise and has distributed leadership throughout the school, ensuring that all teachers receive the support needed. This plan has been used as a model within other schools in the district.	• Has developed a system to identify teachers with expertise to help colleagues address targeted teaching problems, but teachers are unaware of how to secure support • Has not formally measured the degree to which student learning has been impacted as a result of changes in pedagogy resulting from professional learning		
Real-World Examples • *The leader, when asked, identifies at least one colleague at another school within the district whom he or she has personally coached or mentored regarding the goal-setting process.*	• *A majority of teachers indicate that the leaders in this building invite them into discussions to build a collective rather than imposed set of priority goals.* • *A common refrain from teachers in this building is, "leaders in this building listen to my concerns."*	• *Teachers generally agree that leaders in this building are beginning to involve them in the goal-setting discussions.* • *When asked, teachers express mixed views as to the importance of current learning goals*	• *When asked, most teachers indicate that the leaders in this building tend to impose goals and expectations without discussion.* • *A majority of teachers strongly disagree or disagree, with the*

Leading and Participating in Teacher/Leader Learning and Development

• Other leaders in the district credit the leader as a mentor and reason for their success in the goal-setting process. • When asked, the leader is able to articulately describe the process he or she has used to secure feedback as to the effectiveness of the goal-setting process. • The leader is able to provide evidence of how he or she has used the feedback from the goal-setting process to inform next steps.	• A majority of teachers' strongly agree with the importance of the current learning goals. • When asked, most teachers can articulate how what they have now differs from what they truly want, and, thus, the need for change. • When asked, a majority of teachers say that they are clear about the learning goals for which they are responsible. • A majority of teachers feel personally committed to achieving the goals for which they are responsible. • The leader, when asked, can articulate what they have learned from listening to the concerns of others and how that impacted the results of the goal-setting process.	• Many teachers, when asked, are unable to articulate the reason for current learning goals or the need for change. • Teachers express mixed views as to how the goals connect to their day-to-day work. • Fewer than half of the teachers express commitment to the current learning goals.	• importance of the current learning goals. • When asked, a majority of teachers express frustration with the multiple conflicting priorities and work overload. • Most teachers are unclear about expectations and how the goals connect to them personally. • A majority of teachers lack commitment to achieving the goals.

89

Element 5: Providing an Orderly, Safe, and Supportive Environment

T his element is about creating an environment that provides assurance that teachers can focus on teaching along with its impact on student achievement and students can focus on learning. While this element, especially when compared with the four previous instructional leadership elements, makes a rather small but educationally important difference to student achievement (Robinson, 2011), it more importantly enjoys the distinction of being foundational to the other four elements. Think about it this way: strong structures are built on solid foundations, and the leadership of effective schools is no different. It too is built on a solid groundwork of clear and consistently enforced social expectations and discipline codes. The notion of a "foundation" is a powerful metaphor as a way to introduce the last of the five elements of instructional leadership ability. Simply put, as we described and depicted in Chapter 2, any physical structure (i.e., the Egyptian Pyramids, the Temple of Concord in Sicily, the Eiffel Tower) that has been built to last for all time is assembled on a foundation designed to support its structural elements.

Similarly, the framework for instructional leadership ability rests on an equally strong base upon which to support those recognized, research-based, interdependent leadership practices (structural elements). Creating and sustaining a safe and supportive environment is "foundational" to instructional leadership ability "in that although orderliness is not sufficient for a high-quality learning environment, its absence makes the work of educating students practically impossible" (Robinson, 2011, p. 127). Thus, effective leaders work tirelessly on strengthening this essential learning base.

RATIONALE AND DESCRIPTION

Academic achievement and social behavior are highly related (Durlak, Weissburg, Taylor, & Schellinger, 2011). More specifically, researchers have underscored how various interpersonal, instructional, and environmental provisions generate better student and adult performance through the following means: (1) well-established norms of conduct for both students and staff that communicate high expectations and support for academic success, (2) strong teacher-student relationships that cultivate personal commitment to learning and a connectedness to the school, (3) the use of engaging high-impact teaching practices such as class discussion, reciprocal teaching, feedback, and so on. (Hattie, 2012a), in conjunction with proactive classroom management approaches, and (4) safe and orderly environments that promote and reinforce positive classroom behavior. Therefore, effective leaders distinguish themselves from their less-effective counterparts through their work on three specific tasks within this instructional leadership ability element: (1) setting and enforcing clear expectations, (2) protecting teachers from outside pressures, and (3) addressing staff conflict quickly and effectively. Several recent studies have highlighted these key leadership practices. A brief description of each of these three leadership tasks follows.

Task 1: Setting and Enforcing Clear Expectations

In a recent national study of violence in nine Israeli schools, Ron Astor, Rami Benbenishty, and Jose Estrada (2009) discovered that low-violence schools in their study radiated feelings of being safe places. These schools tended to establish and implement disciplinary procedures with great consistency and tended to have a well-defined supervision policy that was clear and fair. Furthermore, the procedures that the leaders and staff of these schools put into place "flowed from the organization and mission of the school" (p. 453). The involvement of the principal was seen as a particularly helpful leadership practice by teachers in helping to ensure consistent approaches to student discipline (Louis et al., 2010). Let us be perfectly clear: peaceful schools anywhere in the world are lead by principals and their leadership teams who have a visible presence in public spaces and who engage in a variety of positive physical and verbal exchanges with students. Teachers in these peaceful schools displayed highly responsible behavior for discipline as they were keenly aware of their students' conduct and responded thoroughly and with personal concern when students acted in a manner that was inconsistent with the established norms. In other words, a critical belief system operating within these schools was a desire to continuously redefine procedures and responsibilities to reduce the potential risk to students throughout the school.

The inclination of leaders at low-violence schools to continuously monitor the quality of the school environment is certainly present in Johanna Lacoe's study (2011) of New York City middle school students, which was designed to investigate student perceptions of their environment. Lacoe found that students who report feeling unsafe in the classroom demonstrate lower performance on tests. Additionally, a large percentage (80%) of the students who reported feeling unsafe in the classroom also felt unsafe in other areas of the school (i.e., hallways, bathrooms, locker rooms, and school grounds). Therefore, leaders who routinely access student voice by asking their students as to their sense of safety in a variety of school arenas as well as gaining their perceptions of bullying and intimidation and then using the information to improve the quality of life in the school may well glean valuable information as to how students are experiencing school so they know what next steps to take to improve upon those conditions. More importantly, leaders who demonstrate that they value student voice through securing this kind of student feedback send powerful messages to students about their commitment to creating and nurturing a safe school environment.

Task 2: Protecting Teachers' Instructional Time and Buffering Teachers From Outside Pressures

Throughout this chapter, we have reinforced the fact that principals have an indirect effect on student achievement through the expert use of various leadership practices associated with being an instructional leader. One such practice is creating a safe and positive school culture by establishing and enforcing clear expectations for students and staff. Another practice, the second task, involves principals preserving teacher's instructional time and buffering teachers from undue pressure from outside influences that might distract them from a coherent course of improvement (Bryk, Sebring, Allensworth, Easton, & Luppescu, 2010).

It is important, however, that you understand what this task is and is not about. This task is about maximizing instructional time for teachers, which requires leaders at times to "mediate the messages that reach teachers from potentially disruptive lobby groups and parents" (Robinson, 2011, p. 126). It also is about leaders creating and refining the systems (i.e., the master schedule, student and staff social and behavioral expectations, etc.) that could, if they are ineffective, steal instructional time from teachers and students. It is not about shutting parents out of being educational partners and being actively involved in the life of the school, especially since parental involvement has consistently be found to be significantly related to gains in student achievement. Other researchers have echoed the conclusions of Bryk et al. (2010) and Robinson (2011) that leaders need to take steps to help teachers focus their time and energy on teaching. For instance, Kenneth Leithwood (2006) in his report to the Elementary Teachers' Federation of Ontario, Canada, suggested that principal leadership that "buffers teachers from disruptions" (p. 18) has a strong influence on teachers' self-efficacy as well as increasing their organizational commitment. Louis et al. (2010) determined from their interviews of teachers and principals that part of the core leadership practice entitled Managing the Instructional Program was "buffering staff from distractions to their work" (p. 75).

So, what does the concept "buffering" actually mean? To begin with, the notion of "buffering" teachers from parents is not about locking parents out of the school. Perhaps the most sensible advice to leaders is that they must work to include parents in the school but at the same time be able to safeguard teachers against the potentially disruptive elements within the parent community. This balancing act that is required of effective principals was nicely described in the research by Michael DiPaola and Megan Tschannen-Moran (2005), who successfully argued that highly effective principals "must engage in both buffering and bridging strategies" (p. 69). The authors described bridging strategies as cooperative strategies (i.e., attendance at PTA meetings, accountability meetings, parent–teacher conferences, sponsor public student performances, and back-to-school nights, etc.) that leaders use to cultivate parental support and involvement. However, given time constraints and the complexity of dealing with multiple constituencies, principals are left to having to make a choice as to how they invest their time. The authors concluded that "bridging strategies are more effective when it comes to fostering student learning" (p. 69).

Task 3: Addressing Staff Conflict Quickly and Effectively

The third task of this last instructional leadership element concerns the issue of conflict management. In general, we define conflict as situations in which people believe they have incompatible goals, interests, principles, or feelings. In light of this definition, conflict within schools is inevitable. Leaders will constantly face situations in which members of their leadership team or staff will almost certainly have ideas about how to address issues that seem incompatible with each other as well as those of the leader. Think about it: faculty members inevitably will have many differences in preferences, style, outlook, assumptions, knowledge, values, and background. Leaders will experience all of these differences and the conflict they induce on a regular basis. Handled well, conflict can be a positive and energizing force within the school, leading to change for the better. Handled poorly, conflict will be destructive, resulting in resentment, low morale, and psychological and physical distress.

Boucher (2013), in a study of seven principals in South Carolina, used a mixed-methods design to evaluate the relationship between conflict management style and school climate. One of the key findings from her investigation was that principals linked the qualities of trust, listening, addressing conflict issues promptly and directly, and self-knowledge to effective management practices. Identifying and resolving conflict early instead of allowing the conflict to fester was strongly associated with improved student achievement. Why? One explanation might be that leaders who are willing to listen to what others have to say, who engage staff in authentic open to learning conversations (Robinson, 2011) and decision making, and who are receptive to teachers expressing concerns and disagreement without fear of reprisal help to build supportive human relationships as these leadership qualities allow people to deal with their differences in productive ways, thereby building trust.

Adding to the importance of trust as a necessary condition for addressing staff conflict quickly and effectively, Bryk et al. (2010) suggested that relational trust is the one method that makes improvement efforts matter by bringing about remedies to "dysfunctional understandings that may now operate among adults and impede educating all children well" (p. 216). In other words, the level of trust that exists among school staff determines how well they work together, solve complex problems, and resolve conflict and therefore affects their ability to positively impact the academic progress of students. According to Robinson (2007), relational trust involves "a willingness to be vulnerable to another party because one has confidence that he or she will fulfill the obligations and expectations relevant to the shared task of education children" (p. 18). The leadership qualities that build relational trust include demonstrating interpersonal respect toward others (e.g., politeness, listening to others with the intent of understanding their concerns, inclusive processes), displaying personal regard for others (e.g., caring for staff), exhibiting role competence (e.g., having an ability to do one's job well, including confronting incompetence), and exhibiting personal integrity (e.g., placing the interests of students ahead of one's own personal and political welfare, match one's words with his or her actions, communicating precisely). Moreover, relational trust is a quality that exists on multiple levels. That is, relational trust is present between school leaders and teachers, between individual teachers, between teachers and parents, and between school leaders and parents. Robinson (2011) posited that the leadership capability of relational trust is joined by two additional capabilities: solving complex problems and applying relevant knowledge—capabilities that all leaders need to possess in order to be effective (Theory of Practice 7).

EVIDENCE OF IMPACT

Leaders provide evidence of their evolving knowledge and skill in the area of ensuring an orderly and safe environment by providing evidence that they are applying the research on setting and enforcing clear expectations, protecting teachers' instructional time, using both bridging strategies and buffering teachers from outside pressures, and addressing staff conflict quickly and effectively. Some examples of how leaders can be shown to demonstrate evidence of impact in this leadership element follow:

- The leader creates multiple opportunities for students to provide feedback about the quality of their classroom and school experience.
- The leader regularly uses surveys to assess students' sense of safety in a variety of in-school and out-of-school arenas as well as their perceptions of bullying and intimidation.
- The leader regularly uses the results from student surveys to improve the quality of school life.
- The leader provides illustrative examples of leaders and/or leadership teams who have moved to redefine procedures and responsibilities designed to continuously reduce the potential risk to students throughout the school.
- Teachers agree that school leaders work to protect teaching time and buffer teaching faculty from distractions to their work.
- Parent involvement efforts are focused on increasing parental engagement with the educational work of the school (Theory of Practice 8).
- The leaders and/or the leadership team evaluates the effectiveness of parent involvement and uses the results of the evaluation to improve those efforts.
- Teachers agree that school leaders address staff conflict quickly and effectively.
- The leader establishes clear and consistently enforced social expectations and discipline codes.

SUMMARY

This element is about creating an environment that provides assurance that teachers, leaders, and students can focus on learning. Inasmuch as this instructional leadership element was presented last and makes a comparatively small but educationally important difference to the student achievement, it is foundational to all of the other elements. We discussed the fact that effective leaders distinguish themselves from their less-effective colleagues through their work on three specific tasks within this element: (1) setting and enforcing clear expectations, (2) protecting teachers' instructional time and buffering teachers from outside pressures, and (3) addressing staff conflict quickly and effectively. Several recent studies were presented in order to highlight the three key leadership practices performed within the fifth instructional leadership element.

Figure 7.1 depicts the rubric for Element 5: "Providing an Orderly, Safe, and Supportive Environment." This rubric, like those for the other elements of instructional leadership ability, consists of three sections. First, we provide rich "word descriptions" of leadership practice that are situated along a continuum ranging from exemplary on one end to not meeting standards on the other. Next, we identify the critical attributes of the element; these critical attributes provide essential guidance for observers as well as those being evaluated in distinguishing between practices at adjacent levels of leadership performance. Last, we present possible real-world examples of what the instructional leadership practice looks like according to the degree of proficiency being practiced in order to invite self-assessment and formative feedback.

Figure 7.1   Rubric for Providing an Orderly, Safe, and Supportive Environment

	Providing an Orderly, Safe, and Supportive Environment			
	Exemplary	**Proficient**	**Progressing**	**Not Meeting Expectations**
Rubric Description	The impact of the leader's actions helps others within the district/school apply the nine Theories of Practice—powerful behaviors, ways of thinking—to their actions, thereby increasing leadership capacity within the district/school.	The impact of the leader's actions is adequate, necessary, and meets the school needs. Actions relevant to this element are appropriate reflections of quality work, with only normal variations.	The impact of the leader's actions reflects performance that shows potential but lacks sufficient proficiencies to improve student learning, instructional practice, and/or other responsibilities.	The impact of the leader's actions demonstrates that he or she either does not understand what is required for proficiency or has demonstrated through his or her action or inaction that he or she chooses not to work toward proficiency.
	In addition to possessing all of the qualities of a "Proficient" leader . . . The leader provides clear, convincing, and consistent evidence that he or she ensures the creation and maintenance of a learning environment in which important academic and social goals can be pursued and achieved by focusing his or her time, knowledge, and skills on three specific tasks within this element. More importantly, the leader helps others throughout the district acquire and use these practices so that they too achieve at the proficient or higher performance levels on this element.	The leader, either directly or through his or her designees, creates an orderly, safe, and supportive environment in which important academic as well as social goals can be pursued and achieved by focusing his or her time, knowledge, and skills on three specific tasks within this element: (1) setting and enforcing clear expectations, (2) protecting teaching time and buffering teachers from outside pressures, and (3) addressing staff conflict quickly and effectively. In an orderly environment, teachers, leaders, and students can focus on learning as their highest priority because clear	The leader understands the importance of creating an environment in which important academic as well as social goals can be pursued and achieved; however, the leader and the leadership team may not be sufficiently focused on one or more of the following tasks within this element: (1) setting and enforcing clear expectations, (2) protecting teaching time and buffering teachers from outside pressures, and (3) addressing staff conflict quickly and effectively. As a result, teachers, leaders, and students struggle to adequately focus on learning as their first priority.	The leader demonstrates little to no understanding of the importance of creating an environment in which important academic as well as social goals can be pursued and achieved. The leader is clearly not focused on, or is unwilling to focus on, critical tasks within this element to guarantee an orderly, safe, and supportive environment. As a result, teachers, leaders, and students are not able to adequately focus their time and energies on learning as the top priority.

	Providing an Orderly, Safe, and Supportive Environment		
	and consistently enforced social expectations and discipline codes have been established.		
The leader involves the school and community to collect data on curricular and extracurricular student involvement to ensure equal opportunity for student participation.	**The leader, either directly or through his or her designees . . .**	**The leader . . .**	**The leader . . .**
The leader . . . • Uses and shares with colleagues how the information collected through the feedback processes (i.e., student, faculty, and parent surveys) are used to improve the learning environment; consequently, can demonstrate how others' leadership performance in this element has also improved • Regularly reviews the need for changes to expectations, structures, rules, and expectations by engaging staff, students, and parents in a dialogue using evaluated data from prior feedback sessions • Often (at least two times per year) serves as a mentor for peers within the district/school in the area of giving and receiving tough messages to improve their knowledge and skill in this area	• Creates multiple (2 or 3) opportunities for students to provide feedback about the quality of their classroom and school experience • Regularly makes use of student surveys as to their sense of safety in a variety of in-school and out-of-school arenas as well as their perceptions of bullying and intimidation • Uses the results from student survey information to improve the quality of school life • Provides multiple (2 or 3) illustrative examples of actions taken that have redefined procedures and responsibilities designed to continuously reduce the potential risk to students throughout the school	• Tends to rely on large-scale survey data only to understand how students view their school experience • Uses the results from student survey information to improve the school environment, but, because the feedback process is infrequent, improvements to safety may not be very timely • Struggles to provide multiple illustrative examples of actions taken to reduce the potential risk to students throughout the school • Understands the importance of buffering teaching faculty from distractions to their work, but efforts are inconsistent • Provides some evidence that parent involvement efforts are focused on increasing	• Is unaware or uninterested in securing student perceptions regarding the school environment • Provides some examples of actions taken to reduce the potential risk to students throughout the school, but these actions tend to be reactionary in nature and not the result of data collection • Does not see the connection between the learning environment and student achievement • Parent involvement efforts are focused on such things as Back-to-School Nights, parent-teacher conferences, award programs, etc. and not necessarily on increasing

Critical Attributes

(*Continued*)

Figure 7.1 (Continued)

Providing an Orderly, Safe, and Supportive Environment		
• Makes certain there are minimal interruptions to teaching time and buffers teaching faculty from distractions to their work • Provides evidence that parent involvement efforts are focused on increasing parental engagement with the educational work of the school • Systematically evaluates the effectiveness of parent involvement and use the results of the evaluation to improve those efforts • Identifies and resolves conflict quickly and effectively rather than allowing it to worsen. • Co-establishes with teachers and students clear and consistently enforced social expectations and discipline codes	parental engagement, but the focus may not be on the educational work of the school and does not evaluate the effectiveness of the leaders' efforts • Demonstrates awareness of potential problems and/or areas of conflict within the school but may not skillfully or quickly resolve the conflict • Has developed schoolwide social expectations and discipline codes; however, they are inconsistently administered	parental engagement with the educational work of the school • Either demonstrates no awareness of potential problems and/or areas of conflict within the school or chooses to tolerate, protect, or avoid confrontation, believing that problems and conflicts will resolve themselves or go away • Expectations are vague and discipline codes tend to be established teacher-by-teacher, resulting in a lack of consistency

Providing an Orderly, Safe, and Supportive Environment

Real-World Examples			
• *The leader, when asked, identifies at least one colleague at another school within the district whom he or she has personally coached or mentored regarding the establishment of an orderly, safe, and supportive environment.* • *Other leaders in the district credit this leader as a mentor and reason for their success in constructive conflict-resolution strategies.* • *"My principal listens deeply to my views, especially when my views differ from her own."* • *"My principal expects high standards and constantly checks to see how he is helping others reach them."*	• *A majority of students surveyed indicate that the leaders in this building invite them into discussions to get a sense of safety in a variety of in-school and out-of-school areas as well as their perceptions of bullying and intimidation.* • *A common refrain from students in this building is, "leaders in this building listen to and use my point of view regarding school safety to improve the learning environment."* • *A majority of teachers strongly agree or agree with the statement that school leaders work to protect teaching time and buffer teachers from distractions to their work.* • *"I can rely upon my school leaders to back me up when I face challenging situations with parents."* • *A majority of surveyed parents strongly agree or agree with the statement that parent involvement efforts are*	• *Students generally agree that leaders in this building are beginning to involve them in safety discussions.* • *A common refrain from students in this building is, "leaders in this building ask for my opinion regarding school safety; however, I am not certain they are using my thoughts to improve the learning environment."* • *When asked, teachers express mixed views whether leaders work to protect instructional time and buffer teachers from outside distractions* • *The leader and/or the leader's designees can demonstrate that they collect parent involvement information but may not be able to show how they are using the data.* • *Teachers express mixed views as to the effectiveness of leaders' efforts to resolve conflict effectively and quickly.*	• *When asked, most students indicate that the leaders in this building do not engage them in discussions about school safety.* • *A common refrain from students in this building is "leaders in this building don't ask for my input regarding school safety."* • *A majority of teachers strongly disagree or disagree with the statement, "leaders in this building work to protect instructional time and buffer teachers from outside distractions."* • *The leader is unable to demonstrate that he or she collects, let alone uses, parent involvement information.* • *When asked, most teachers indicate that school leaders take a hands-off approach*

(Continued)

Figure 7.1 (Continued)

Providing an Orderly, Safe, and Supportive Environment

	focused on increasing parental engagement with the educational work of the school. • The leader and/or the leader's designees, when asked, can articulate how the results of the parent involvement evaluation have been used to improve future efforts in this area. • A majority of teachers strongly agree or agree that school leaders address staff conflict quickly and effectively. • A common refrain from teachers in this building is, "I feel free to discuss work problems with my principal without fear of it being used against me later." • "My school leaders communicate and consistently enforces clear expectations, structures, and fair rules and procedures for students and staff."	• "My principal communicates rules and procedures to students and staff. However, the rules are applied inconsistently."	to dealing with staff conflict and simply allow problems to worsen. • "My principal develops and communicates procedures for students and staff."

Feedback for Learning

This chapter addresses the importance of feedback to learning for school leaders, the manner in which feedback is given and secured between the participants within the evaluation cycle to prompt active information processing and application, and the impact of feedback on the participants that leads to enhanced leadership and instructional practices. Why devote an entire chapter to the topic of feedback? Simply put, "feedback significantly improves learning" (Wiliam, 2012, p. 32), regardless of whether it is the learning of adolescents or the learning of adults. Feedback is critical to all learning.

Think back for a moment to the childhood game in which you hide an object and provide clues such as "You're cold! Now you're getting warmer! Warmer! You're HOT!" Young children playing the popular "Hot or Cold" game know that to perform well (that is, to find the hidden object), they need to receive feedback on how they are doing and they need to use the information to make adjustments to their search efforts in order to achieve the goal of finding the object. Without feedback, they are literally walking blind. If they are lucky, they will accidentally reach their goal. If not, they will find themselves wandering aimlessly through the dark, never reaching their destination. Just as feedback is critical in order for children to achieve the goal of the game, specific and timely feedback is an essential component of any effective appraisal system and should be used in conjunction with setting clear learning intentions and success criteria. If feedback is provided to as well as secured from employees on their progress towards their learning intentions, employee performance, like student performance, will improve.

In our work with clients across the nation, a common refrain among leaders is that, although they understand the importance of feedback, they do not have the time to give or to secure feedback to improve his or her impact on others. In other words, these individuals do not have time to use feedback about their practice to improve their own learning. This phenomenon could be likened to a physician who refuses to use the latest findings in medicine to improve his or her practices when treating patients. In fact, physicians who practice with outdated methods could easily be charged with malpractice. In a similar fashion, educational leaders who refuse to use high-effect-size practices to increase learning—that is, the best practices according to the research—could be guilty of educational malpractice. According to Grant Wiggins (2012), decades of education research support the idea that "less teaching plus more feedback equals better results" (p. 13).

Just as high-performing teachers collect both formative and summative feedback to modify and differentiate their instructional practices based on the needs of their students, so too does the high-performing school leader adjust his or her practices based on the needs of his or her teachers. Therefore, knowing that we all want better results and that effective feedback is a proven strategy toward that end, let's look closely at what the research is telling us regarding the effect of feedback on learning, how district and school leaders are changing how they view their roles, and how they secure and use feedback to adjust their leadership practices. While most of the feedback research that we will be citing focuses on practices used in classrooms or what happens between teachers and students, we believe that we can, with a high degree of confidence, make the assumption that when feedback practices are used in a very similar manner between central office leaders and principals, it is equally as powerful. In support of the assumption that what works for adolescent learners also works for adult learners, the National Research Council (2000), in the book entitled *How People Learn: Brain, Mind, Experience, and School*, concluded that:

> The principles of learning and their implications for designing learning environments apply equally to child, adolescent, and adult learning. They provide a lens through which current practice can be viewed with respect to K-12 teaching and with respect to preparation of teachers in research and development agenda. The principles are relevant as well when we consider other groups, such as policy makers and the public, whose learning is also required for educational practice to change. (p. 27)

FEEDBACK: WHAT THE RESEARCH REVEALS

To understand what the research reveals about feedback, we want to begin by defining the term. Although we thought that this would be a relatively easy concept to find in the research, our search actually found many different definitions as well as writings on feedback that failed to define the term, perhaps assuming that feedback is a universally understood concept.

Professor Hattie (2009), whose ground-breaking evidence-based research includes more than 50,000 studies and more than 1,000 meta-analyses, looked into what actually works best in schools to improve learning. Hattie found that feedback is one of the most powerful influences on how people learn, yet he acknowledged that he himself has "struggled to understand the concept" (p. 173). Additionally, Hattie and Timperley (2007) noted that while feedback is frequently mentioned and described in research articles and books about teaching and learning, few recent studies have systematically investigated its meaning.

In their article entitled *The Power of Feedback* (2007), Hattie and Timperley defined feedback as "information provided by an agent (e.g., teacher, peer, book, parent, self, experience) regarding aspects of one's performance or understanding" (p. 81), which reduces the gap between the student's current level of understanding and/or performance and the goal. Depending on the nature and delivery of the feedback, it can have powerful positive effects on student learning and engagement. The research also clearly revealed that while the impact of feedback on learning and achievement is high, the type of feedback, the way in which it is given, and what the learner does with the information can have very different effects, indicating that not all feedback supports learning. As Stiggins, Arter, Chappuis, and Fung (2004) pointed out, "It's the quality of the feedback rather than its existence or absence that determines its power" (p. 40). Feedback needs to be structured to identify for the learner what was done well, what needs improvement, and how to improve (Black, Harrison, Lee, & William, 2003; Hattie & Timperley, 2007). Just as Hattie's (2009) comprehensive meta-analysis of the influences on student achievement, which mainly focused on learners between the ages of 4 and 20 years, revealed that feedback has an overall effect size of 0.75, we can, with a fairly reliable claim, state that this research would also hold true for adult learners as well. Additionally, we know that feedback is not just confined to teachers and students in the classroom setting. Professor Hattie (2009), in considering the role of feedback in self-regulation and lifelong learning, helps us all to understand that there are huge benefits to learning, regardless of age, if we all know when to seek feedback, know how to seek feedback, and know what to do with feedback when we get it. The research findings on feedback provide us with a set of benchmarks that can be used to create debates, to seek evidence, and to self-review to determine whether a leader is having a marked impact on all students. This research highlights the importance of educators as evaluators of their impact.

As a professional, it is critical for you to know your impact (Hattie, 2009). It may seem contradictory, but the more leaders pursue feedback about their own effect on others, the more benefits accrue to their teachers directly and to their students indirectly. However, as Viviane Robinson (2011) pointed out, this may not always be the case as many times the feedback that leaders seek about their leadership practices does not include inquiries into the impact on student learning. For example, in many of the state and local evaluation systems that we researched for this book, we discovered that, overall, school leadership is judged by such things as the quality of management, leaders' relationships with the adults in the system, and the number of high-profile innovations in place within the school. Additionally, evaluators within these leadership-evaluation systems are seeking, receiving, and providing to principals feedback regarding happy and well-behaved children; the amount of parent involvement and concerns received; the appropriateness of how financial resources are being used; the level of their popularity among staff, parents, and district officials; and whether or not school leaders are showcased in their community as effective leaders. While the findings reported by Robinson et al. (2008) clearly indicate that excellent school management is an important leadership quality, it should not be confused with leadership effectiveness, as it is entirely possible to have well-managed schools with highly motivational school leaders and inspired staff who collaborate to overcome challenges but still have students performing below where they need to or should be.

In contrast, our principal-evaluation framework will measure the frequency and quality of the use of research-based high-effect-size leadership practices and the impact and difference these practices are making to the learning within the school and to student achievement. Evaluators will give and secure frequent and ongoing feedback that will be both formative and summative in nature. The first type, formative feedback, will be used and collected from a variety of sources to inform school leaders of their ongoing impact and application of their leadership practices. The second type, summative feedback, which is designed to measure the overall impact of the leader on teacher effectiveness and student achievement, as well as other measures, will be used at the end of the year to determine overall leadership impact. The first type, formative feedback, will be the focus of this chapter. So, we ask ourselves, why is formative feedback so powerful?

To answer this question, we look to the research on feedback that explicitly shows that districts that provide effective feedback to educators on the impact that they are having or not having on student achievement, that foster a culture that is focused on improvement along with a willingness to seek evidence of leaders' impact, and that have an openness to new ideas and strategies are seeing increases in student achievement (Hattie & Yates, 2014). While we can give many personal examples of the use of effective formative feedback, we would like to take our readers vicariously to Shelbyville, Kentucky, to showcase the exceptional feedback practices of a colleague with whom we have worked.

Shelby County School District

Community members view Mr. James Neihof, Superintendent of Shelby County School District, as both a transformational as well as an instructional leader who has a laser-like focus on student achievement. In fact, their mission is to "Think Big," and Mr. Neihof is thinking big as he asked the state department of education if he could modify and enhance the state-mandated Principal Professional Growth and Effectiveness System (PPGES) on the basis of his work with us in the area of leaders' growth plans. Specifically, the modification to their existing growth plan would provide a framework for all district and school leaders to have a stronger focus on instructional leadership by regularly monitoring data on both cause (i.e., the actions of adults) and effect (i.e., the impact on student achievement). In other words, the data on cause would provide feedback regarding direct leadership impact on the adults in the system, and the data on effect would show the indirect impact that leaders were having on student achievement. Mr. Neihof wants his leaders to "know thy impact" (Hattie, 2009, p. 169) by selecting a main focus and by engaging principals in monthly self-monitoring of leadership actions against student achievement results in order to create greater teacher and leader efficacy. The modified PPGES is called a Plan on a Page (POP) by Shelby County and is very similar to what we have previously defined and clearly described in Chapter 8. An example of a Shelby County POP plan can be found in the appendix.

As an instructional leader, Mr. Neihof knows the power of feedback as a tool for improving learning and has therefore embedded the POP feedback process district-wide. In the first year in which POP plans were written, principals received feedback from Mr. Neihof and from their supervisors based on the established success criteria, a POP development rubric (i.e., similar to the Deliberate Practice Development Rubric that we describe in Chapter 10), to gauge whether the plan was effectively written. Once the plan meets the established criteria, district and school leaders use an implementation rubric (i.e., similar to the Deliberate Practice Implementation Rubric that we describe in Chapter 10) as a feedback tool to gather specific and timely information from leaders, staff, and students to inform the leader's decisions to maintain the focus and practices or to monitor and adjust on the basis of the feedback received.

School leaders not only continue to share their POP plans monthly at staff meetings, thereby providing feedback to teachers regarding the impact of adult practices on student achievement (cause and effect data), they also share their plans with other principal colleagues at regular intervals throughout the year. The sharing of POP plans with other colleagues is focused on feedback that is specific to the implementation of leadership practices and tasks that the leader has outlined in his or her POP plan and puts an emphasis on the learning goals (Kluger & DeNisi, 1996). In giving each other descriptive feedback, principals model the kind of thinking you want them to exhibit as self-regulators of their own learning. The overall effects of the use of peers as co-teachers (of themselves and of others) in classes are, generally, quite powerful. If the aim is to teach students (and in this case, leaders) self-regulation skills and control over their own learning, then they must move from being students of their effects to being teachers of their learning (Hattie, 2009). This ongoing, specific, and timely formative feedback around leadership practices and the impact on student learning is informing Shelby County School leaders about the effect that their leadership practices are having on student achievement. In a recent conversation (personal communication, April 28, 2014), Mr. Neihof said that, "It has been exciting to see…school leaders embrace the POP process and to grow in their understanding of the power of collecting both cause and effect data to determine the impact of their leadership practices."

Mr. Neihof, while pleased with the results that this leadership practice is yielding, already is making plans for how he might spread the practice even further within his school district. He intends to broaden the POP planning process to include other district/school leaders and teachers in subsequent years. There is a significant body of research on the impact of feedback on both learning and motivation. It is our intent that this brief analysis of the research will provide for our readers a conceptual analysis of feedback and a framework that leaders can use to measure their impact on learning and achievement.

WHAT CONSTITUTES EFFECTIVE FEEDBACK?

As we have cited earlier, feedback is information that is provided by someone or something concerning the qualities of one's practice or actions (Hattie & Timperley, 2007). For instance, an evaluator can provide feedback to a principal, or a colleague/peer could provide an alternate strategy to the principal, or a teacher could provide the principal focused feedback on his or her leadership impact in the school, or a community member could provide parental insights, or a principal could use the Internet or a book or article to check his or her understanding regarding an instructional practice to help clarify ideas and understandings. Simply put, feedback can come from a variety of sources. The information shared becomes feedback if, and only if, the learner is trying to cause something to happen and the information tells him or her whether he or she is on track or needs to change course.

The purpose of feedback is to reduce discrepancies between current understandings, performance, and the learning goal or target (Hattie & Timperley, 2007). To close this learning gap, it is critical that school leaders first have a clear goal in mind and know the success criteria (what the leadership practice looks like when performed at the proficient and higher levels) and knows how well they are doing toward that goal. As outlined in the feedback model described by Hattie and Timperley (2007), feedback should answer three questions for the leader: *Where am I going? How am I going? Where to next?* Feedback that answers the first question, *Where am I going?*, affirms the learning goal and what success would look like to accomplish this goal. This type of feedback tells the leader specifically what he or she needs to improve in order to accomplish the goal. For example, a learning goal for a school principal could fall under Instructional Leadership Ability Element 4: "Leading and Participating in Teacher/ Leader Learning and Development." Specifically, the leader might set a goal of increasing the percentage of teachers who are using effective feedback practices during classroom instruction at the proficient or higher levels from 20% to 75%.

The second question is *How am I going?* Feedback that answers this question tells the leader what progress he or she is making toward accomplishing the learning goal. It provides information on such things as what teachers understand and where they are confused regarding the use of effective feedback. For example, after a scheduled professional development session on the topic of feedback, the leader engages his or her faculty in meaningful dialogue on key learning intentions achieved. That is, the leader might request feedback from teachers regarding their understanding of the specific effective feedback strategies that were taught during the session, which concepts are clear, which concepts need further explanation, and their plan to implement one or two of the strategies in the upcoming week. This individualized teacher feedback will let the principal know the depth of understanding from the training regarding the strategies taught and the ability of the teachers to apply their learning in the classroom. Additionally, this feedback will give both the principal and his or her teachers insights into where they currently are in relationship to the goal.

The third question is, *Where to next?* Feedback that answers this question helps leaders to know where they are supposed to go next as they work toward goal attainment (75% of staff implementing effective feedback at the proficient or higher levels). Specifically, where should the leader put his or her time, effort, and attention in order to close the gap between the goal and existing faculty performance levels? Using our same example, once the principal had an understanding of the degree to which his or her teachers had acquired the knowledge and skills to implement effective feedback strategies from the original professional development session, the leader could determine his or her next steps in differentiating the learning for their teachers. To understand the power of using these three feedback questions to guide leadership practices, let's see how these practices might actually look in the real world by taking you to Broward County School District in Fort Lauderdale, Florida, and the feedback process that Keith Peters, principal at Gator Run Elementary School, developed to inform and modify his leadership practices.

Gator Run Elementary School

In an effort to ascertain the climate of his school and to determine teachers' level of expertise with specific instructional strategies, Keith instituted a quarterly teacher survey. The survey served the dual purpose of collecting needed data while also causing teachers to self-reflect on their instructional practice. In order to answer the question, *Where are we going?*, this year the school focused on the implementation of collaborative grouping as a strategy. The goal was to see a higher level of student engagement by creating opportunities for the children to work together to solve problems and/or create solutions. Keith wanted teachers to provide instruction and guidance on how students could work together collaboratively. Keith used Survey Monkey as a means of collecting feedback from his staff on their understanding of and skill at proficiently implementing various collaborative grouping strategies.

To answer the question, *How are we going?*, quarterly teacher survey results showed an increase of skill among the teachers about implementing this strategy, with the percentage of teachers responding with either "I could teach others" or "comfortable" increasing from 52% at the beginning of the year to 74% at the middle of the year and to 82% at the end of the year. In a phone conversation (personal communication, April 2, 2014), Keith commented that,

> As beneficial as these results are, even better are the remarks that teachers write in the comments section. While there are numerous positive comments stating that we are heading in the right direction, I gain the most from those comments that provide direct, specific feedback. I have learned that sometimes my message has not been clear, that teachers need additional support and training, and that sometimes my perception is not accurate. This feedback has informed my practice and caused genuine change in how I run my school. I am a big believer in feedback, both providing it to others and receiving it as well. This, in turn, has made me a better leader, a better coach, and a better person.

As a result, Keith has the answer to the third question, *Where to next?*, which is helping him to close the gap between the established goal and the current practice of his teachers.

Our Instructional Leadership Ability evaluation framework and rubrics provide the goal and the success criteria along with information shared from various agents such as teachers, school leaders, and central office leaders in the form of real-world examples. This type of specific and ongoing feedback helps the leader to become keenly aware of what he or she knows and can do, what he or she does not know and cannot do, what he or she knows so well that they can teach others, and what feedback he or she can use to refine their own skills. Thus, armed with this feedback, leader can proceed to reduce the discrepancies between current understandings, performance, and their learning goals. Evaluators need to clarify with the leader a clear understanding of what constitutes successful achievement of the learning goals (i.e., the critical attributes) and link their feedback directly to the learning or performance goals. Furthermore, by expressing what leaders are expected to know and be able to do and what it looks like to accomplish these goals, we empower leaders with the ability to engage in self-regulation practices—to monitor their own progress and to continually set and reset their individual learning goals.

In summary, for feedback to be more effective, leaders need to make sure that they have clarified their learning and/or performance goals (refer to Chapter 3 for a detailed description of the difference between learning and performance goals), are continually seeking and securing specific and timely feedback regarding their performance, and are using the information to prioritize their time, effort, and attention. Feedback must answer three important questions: (1) *Where am I going?* (2) *How am I going?* and (3) *Where to next?* Last, the feedback secured by the leader provides the leader with information to help him or her enhance or modify his or her leadership practices. The research clearly denotes that the three questions do not stand alone but work together in a iterative cycle of understanding the goals, working out progress toward them, and identifying better strategies for achieving their goals.

THE FOUR LEVELS OF FEEDBACK

Hattie and Timperley (2007), in their model of feedback, show how the three questions, *Where am I going?*, *How am I going?*, and *Where to next?* influence feedback at four different levels: (1) the *Task Level*, (2) the *Process Level*, (2) the *Self-Regulation Level*, and the (4) *Self Level*. The first three levels can all have powerful impacts on learning; however, the fourth level of feedback is about the self as a person and is seen as least effective (Hattie & Timperley, 2007). Feedback aimed at the self is usually less effective as it rarely provides information about the three questions and typically consists of personal evaluations and praise regarding the character of the learner.

As coaches and evaluators of school leaders, it is important to understand that feedback will look somewhat different depending on the level of knowledge and skills being demonstrated by the school leader. Feedback at the *Task Level* is generally provided to someone who is early in the learning cycle (a novice learner) and includes information about how well a task was being performed or supporting the learner by providing more information, or different content, or correcting a misunderstanding he or she might have about the content. Feedback of this nature clearly delineates what the learner needs to do to improve his or her performance on the task. Suppose, for instance, a school leader's understanding of his or her role in improving the effectiveness of his or her teachers (Instructional Leadership Ability Element 4) regarding their professional development is limited to the practice of scheduling, securing and paying for the presenter, preparing a location, providing refreshments, and seeing to it that teachers have the hand-outs, and so on. In other words, the leader makes all of the arrangements for and handles the managerial aspects of the professional development in which teachers will engage but does not personally participate in the professional development along with their teachers. The feedback that this leader's supervisor might provide could sound like this, *"Your goal is to not only promote the professional development of your teachers, which you have done, but it also includes you participating with and at times leading the professional learning of your teachers. The next time you schedule a professional learning opportunity for your teachers, you need to make certain that you fully participate along with your teachers in that learning opportunity and not drop in and out of the workshop."* Other examples of feedback at the Task Level are reflected in Figure 8.1.

Figure 8.1   Examples of Feedback at the Task Level

Example	Task Level Feedback Examples
1	*You were present during the teachers' professional learning day; however, you sat in the back of the room and responded to emails. Your physical presence is important but insufficient—you need to sit with staff, participate in the process, and listen to them learning so that you will know how best to support them during implementation.*
2	*Hmm. Think about the qualities for effective professional learning we reviewed last week. As I listen to your planning for your in-service day, two of those qualities have not been addressed. Can you fix that?*

Feedback at the *Process Level* is about the processing of the task and provides comments or information about the processes that the school leader is using to perform the task or to develop the product. Specifically, feedback at this level is about strategies that the leader might use to detect and learn from errors and that will provide insights or information that will help him or her to establish relationships among and between ideas. Suppose now, however, that the school leader in the previous example is showing progress in his or her learning about the leader's role in improving the effectiveness of teachers (Instructional Leadership Ability Element 4). That is, the leader understands that this role includes both promoting and participating in teachers' professional learning opportunities. In this case, the supervisor's feedback to the school leader might sound something like this: *"What strategies might you use to determine how effective the professional learning offering was for your staff?"* Additional examples of feedback at the Process Level are depicted in Figure 8.2.

The third level of feedback, *Self-Regulation*, addresses the way in which learners regulate, monitor, and direct their own learning toward a goal.

Figure 8.2   Examples of Feedback at the Process Level

Example	Process Level Feedback Examples
1	*How could you use the feedback that you received from your faculty after your last professional learning event to make certain that this new event goes smoothly?*
2	*How could you use the exemplar Mike shared with us during our last principals' meeting to help you structure your professional learning work?*

At this level, the feedback helps the individual assume a great deal of autonomy, self-regulation, and self-control over his or her learning. That is, feedback at this level helps the learner to become the driver of his or her own learning. Continuing with our example, a school leader who has demonstrated a high-degree of proficiency with Element 4 and who is showing improved understanding about the leader's role in improving the effectiveness of teachers should receive feedback from their supervisor like this: *"How are you thinking about monitoring the degree to which teachers are practicing what they learned during their professional development?"* Additional examples of feedback at the Self-Regulation Level are represented in Figure 8.3.

Figure 8.3   Examples of Feedback at the Self-Regulation Level

Example	Self-Regulation Level Feedback Examples
1	*Maya, I am going to ask you to reflect on your last professional learning event. What are some of the key suggestions that you would advise other principals to follow next time if you were teaching about conducting a successful professional learning event?*
2	*Thanks, Juan, I would really appreciate you giving Fabian some feedback that he could consider for monitoring teachers' implementation of skills that they learned in a professional learning seminar.*

To achieve maximum benefit, supervisors of school leaders should strive to provide information (feedback) that moves him or her from task to processing and then from processing to self-regulation. Hattie (2009) believes that engaged and passionate teachers strive to be students of their own influence at the same time assisting students to be teachers of their own learning. We believe the same expectation should be made of highly effective school leaders. These leaders are those who develop the disposition to be students of their own effects and develop within their teachers the capacity to become teachers of their own learning. The key is for supervisors of school leaders to have a strong understanding of the level of competency of the leader relative to the five elements of instructional leadership ability. Moreover, the goal for supervisors when working with school leaders is to use effective feedback practices focused around these five elements to support leaders in obtaining the knowledge and mastering the skills needed to have a significant impact on both adult and student learning within their school. Just as teachers must keep their students focused on learning goals and success criteria (Hattie, 2009), effective supervisors must keep school leaders focused on learning goals (i.e., the five elements) and success criteria (i.e., the rubrics) or leadership practices that, when implemented with fidelity, should yield a high degree of impact on teacher effectiveness and student achievement.

The final level of feedback is called *Self* feedback. While this sort of feedback is usually ineffective at advancing learning as it contains almost no task, process, or self-regulation feedback-related information and is rarely connected to a specific learning goal, Hattie and Timperley (2007) included it as a level because of the high frequency of its use in classrooms. For instance, a comment from a supervisor to a principal such as, *"You really did a bang-up job with that professional development the other day!"* leaves the principal wondering what exactly she or he did that was so good (i.e., what specific leadership knowledge and/or skills did the leader exhibit)? What precisely did the leader do that contributed to effective professional development? This type of positive or negative information is about the learner as a person and usually directs the learner's attention away from the learning goal and onto what the person thinks of the learner as an individual. However, personal feedback that assists in enhancing the leader's effort, engagement, or feelings of self-efficacy, such as, *"You really did a bang-up job with that professional development the other day because you committed your full attention to the learning even though you had other pressing matters!"* may impact the leader's learning.

As noted by Professor Hattie (2012b), feedback from the student to the teacher is essential to learning. We can make a similar conclusion that feedback between the supervisor and the school leader is most effective when the school leader provides feedback to the evaluator about what the leader knows, what he or she understands, where he or she is having problems, and how he or she likes to learn. This ongoing dialogue between the evaluator and the school leader keeps a laser-like focus on the specific learning goals to help close the gap between the current practice and the desired goal. Feedback that is given to supervisors from school leaders, just like the feedback that is given to teachers from students, works to make learning visible (Hattie, 2009) for both the supervisor as well as the leader.

To share a personal story, when we were exploring and researching the concept of principal socialization into school districts—the topic of our dissertations (Smith, J. R., 2007; Smith, R. L., 2007)—and the kind of support that leaders received during their first three years as new administrators, principals overwhelmingly reported that they were largely hired, given the keys, and left alone. Supervisors provided little to no task, process, or self-regulation feedback that principals could use to improve their leadership performance. Moreover, when principals did receive feedback, it was rarely connected to specific learning goals and success criteria and felt more like advice, or praise, or criticism. The most common form of feedback reported by school leaders occurred during their biannual reviews, during which overall evaluation ratings were shared and leaders received either personal tributes or condemnations regarding their performance on very broad district-wide goals.

A CULTURE FOR FEEDBACK

Professor Hattie (2012b), in his article entitled "Know Thy Impact," noted that "feedback thrives in conditions of error of not knowing—not in environments where we already know and understand" (p. 23). Thus, district supervisors need to welcome error in a similar fashion that a teacher would welcome error and misunderstanding from students in their classrooms. School leaders may come to their new position with incorrect or poorly developed understandings of certain leadership practices, and these misconceptions could become major barriers to their success as school leaders if they do not feel safe in asking questions and seeking out feedback. In order for this to happen, there needs to be a culture and environment of trust.

For example, take a moment and ask yourself what is something you once believed to be true in your work but no longer believe to be true based on new information? When we asked this question of school district leaders with whom we work, many noted that they believed, as a result of their school observations, that they were giving leaders good feedback. Generally speaking, the core understanding of feedback for many school district leaders has been very linear, with feedback being provided in the form of comments, advice, or suggestions to the teachers whom they were evaluating, with little or no thought given to the specific learning intentions, success criteria, and levels of feedback based on the leader's degree of competency. We would also like to point out that the same statement can be made of school leaders as they observe teachers in classrooms and offer feedback. Consequently, school district leaders who are not aware of the practices associated with effective feedback might have been giving leaders feedback that was not seen as being supportive. Once these district officials developed a deeper understanding of what constitutes effective feedback, many indicated that they no longer believed that their past practice reflected effective feedback practice and were moving to change their leadership practices. More importantly, changes in leadership practice that result in improved relations with leaders help to build relational trust.

From personal experiences, we all know that we learn most easily in an environment wherein we trust the individuals with whom we are working, and the system in which we are working, to ask questions and receive feedback without fearing negative reactions or consequences from our peers or supervisors. Understanding and using effective feedback is not as simple as merely reading the research, checking steps off a list, and declaring that we now provide "effective feedback." There needs to be a culture throughout the school that is welcoming of feedback and of making errors. Bryk and Schneider (2003), in a longitudinal study of 400 elementary schools in Chicago, determined that while trust alone does not guarantee success, schools with little or no trust have almost no chance of improving. They likened the idea of relational trust to the "connective tissue that binds individuals together" (p. 45) to promote the well-being of students and staff. In order for feedback to thrive in our schools and school districts, it is necessary for teacher–teacher, teacher–principal, and supervisor–principal relationships to be based on a foundation of trust. Relational trust is a byproduct of four conditions (Bryk & Schneider, 2003). First, highly effective leaders build trust by being willing to genuinely listen to others' opinions and seek others' points of view (an essential condition within the feedback literature), even when people disagree, and yet still help people to feel valued. Second, leaders who demonstrate strong personal regard for others build relational trust. Third, staff and community members want to feel as if their interactions with one another are producing expected results. The attainment of this feeling is based in large part on the school district and/or school leader's ability to fairly and skillfully manage basic school and district operations. Fourth, the district/school leader must be able to align his or her words with his or her actions. That is, the leader must demonstrate personal integrity. Trust is broken when individuals hear the leader saying one thing and yet practicing something entirely different.

USING FEEDBACK TO DEVELOP LEADERS' SELF-REGULATION SKILLS

Chappuis (2005), in her Educational Leadership article entitled "Helping Students Understand Assessment" noted, "In giving students descriptive feedback, you have modeled the kind of thinking you want them to do as self-assessors" (p. 41). With this thought in mind, the key question we find ourselves asking is how can supervisors of leaders use feedback practices to help school leaders develop self-regulation skills and become independent learners and in return have these leaders model and support the similar behaviors for teachers? Let's return to Hattie's (2012a) three questions: *Where am I going? How am I going?* and *Where to next?* Helping leaders identify the learning intentions and success criteria so that they can determine what is being done well, what needs to improve, and what next steps to take is critical to self-regulation. Early on, as school leaders are developing as independent learners and learning new leadership practices, they will rely more heavily on their supervisor for feedback regarding next steps. During this time, the supervisor uses feedback not only to provide direction and focus for the leader but also to teach and explicitly model the skills of self-regulation and goal-setting so that the leader can become more independent and drive his or her own learning.

HOW CAN SUPERVISORS MAKE FEEDBACK MORE EFFECTIVE?

Just as school leaders must create a culture that is failure-tolerant, supervisors too need to create a culture that welcomes feedback—one in which relational trust and learning are at the heart of the work. Errors need to be welcomed, as feedback is most effective when learners do not have proficiency or mastery. Supervisors need to clearly articulate the learning intentions (goals) and success criteria in order to close the gap between where the school leaders are and where they should be. Therefore, supervisors need to know what each leader brings to the school/district and what successful leadership practices look like according to descriptive rubrics of leadership practices. Additionally, supervisors need to ensure that leaders understand the feedback and are able to take the next step. Many times, supervisors give feedback but the principal does not receive it and therefore use it to change his or her practice. A simple strategy for ensuring that school leaders have received the supervisor's feedback might be to ask the leader to summarize the feedback that he or she received and what his or her next steps might be. Another strategy to make certain that leaders are receiving feedback and are using the feedback to alter leadership practices is for supervisors to use a Feedback Response Sheet with school leaders (see Figure R.2 in the "Resources" section for an example). The Feedback Response Sheet enables the supervisor to provide descriptive feedback to the school leader based on the success criteria (i.e., the descriptions of proficient leadership behavior) and then have the leader comment on how he or she intends to incorporate that feedback into future practice.

Supervisors also need to remember that feedback is not linear but multidimensional, meaning that supervisors not only should give feedback to school leaders but also should seek feedback from school leaders. Consequently, supervisors need to have a system for collecting feedback from school leaders. This form of feedback enables supervisors to make adjustments in their leadership practices, which in turn causes leaders to adapt content, tasks, and/or strategies toward new learning intentions. Peer feedback also should be embedded in the feedback process whereby supervisors of school leaders create opportunities for pairs and teams of school leaders to come together to observe each other in action in schools and to talk about strategies and practices for improving their leadership practices. Similar to teachers who have professional learning communities (PLCs) to discuss student learning, districts would set up PLCs for school leaders to talk about learning in their schools.

Just as principals need to spend time in their classrooms to be able to give timely and meaningful feedback regarding instructional practices, it is equally important for supervisors to spend time in schools in order to provide and seek feedback and to give support. Successful monitoring practices revolve around three qualities. First, the monitoring should be frequent; we suggest that supervisors have a minimum of three to five interactions with principals throughout the year. Second, the monitoring should be focused on adult actions. Just as leaders need to continue to collect student (effect) data, they also need to collect adult (cause) data. That is, "How are the instructional and/or leadership practices impacting student achievement?" Third, the monitoring should be constructive. As Reeves (2011) warned, supervisors of leaders have the option of conducting either a "witch hunt" or a "treasure hunt" (p. 30). A witch hunt consists of school/classroom observations that are characterized by leaders going into schools and classrooms armed with lengthy checklists with the intention of identifying what the leader is missing. This sort of game of *Defect Detection!* promotes an adversarial relationship between the supervisor and the school leader and works to undermine efforts to build relational trust. In contrast, a "treasure hunt" approach is one in which the supervisor has a list of clearly identified prioritized instructional/leadership practices (learning intentions and success criteria) that he or she expects the school leader to effectively and systematically implement into his or her leadership practice and therefore needs feedback on what is observed.

USING FEEDBACK WITHIN THE EVALUATION FRAMEWORK

We have learned a great deal about feedback and have begun to understand that it is not a linear, one-way process whereby feedback is only provided by one person to another. Rather, feedback is multidimensional as well as multidirectional. There are a number of sources for leaders to receive feedback within our evaluation framework. For instance, a school leader could receive feedback from his or her direct supervisor, or from peers and from their staff, or from an educational article, or from an evaluation rubric. Mr. Tucker Harris, an assistant principal at Pine Trail Elementary School in Volusia County Schools, has put into place an excellent example of how feedback is nonlinear and flows from many different sources.

Pine Trail Elementary School

This year, as part of his Florida School Leader Assessment evaluation process, Tucker was determined to focus on improving his instructional leadership practices with a specific emphasis on leadership indicators under *Faculty Development,* which included leading professional learning and improving the percentage of highly effective teachers on his faculty. After Tucker attended a professional learning session on providing effective feedback to teachers, he had an "Aha" moment when he realized that the feedback that he was personally missing regarding his own leadership impact on teachers was the feedback from the teachers themselves. As a result, Tucker said (personal correspondence, April 10, 2014) that he was inspired to do the following:

> I asked myself the three guiding questions to inform my leadership practice. The question that relates to how I am doing kept popping up in my mind. I could not think of any time I received feedback regarding my practice as a facilitator of professional learning. To address this area of need, I developed a brief professional learning opportunity that differentiated between feedback and praise. I presented the faculty with the professional learning and concluded the faculty meeting with a survey I developed with the assistance from a primary teacher at Pine Trail Elementary. The survey was developed using an online format and was anonymous. The survey asked the following questions: 1) What am I doing that is having an impact on your teaching and/or learning? 2) What am I doing that is interfering with your teaching and/or learning? I plan to take the results from the survey to use as follow up training with the faculty by projecting examples and allowing the faculty to read and identify as feedback or praise. For the items identified as praise, I will ask the faculty to rewrite the *praise statements* with the attributes of effective feedback. The results will then be used to help me decide what I will continue with my practice, what I will discard, and what I will add. This practice not only provides me with the critical feedback needed to improve my practice as it relates to faculty development, but more importantly builds trust with the faculty.

In our correspondence with Tucker (personal communication, April 10, 2014), he was amazed at how receptive his staff was in giving him feedback. Tucker received comments such as those reflected in Figure 8.4.

These comments from teachers not only validated the work that he was doing with his staff to build trusting relationships but also, more importantly, provided him with specific feedback needed to reflect on his own leadership practices in order to determine what next steps he needed to take to fill in the gap between the needs improvement and proficient leadership performance—the learning intention.

Mr. Harris's actions take us back to something that Grant Wiggins (2012) wrote about in his article "Seven Keys to Effective Feedback" regarding the universal outcry from teachers that there is just no time for giving feedback. To this, Wiggins stated that, "no time to give and use feedback actually

Figure 8.4   Select Teacher Comments

> "You give immediate feedback on lessons observed that is beneficial. You are also very supportive of the staff and you offer support wherever and when needed. Our concerns are not pushed aside."

> "The professional development you are presenting is clear, concise and HOLDING US ACCOUNTABLE...YAY!"

> "I like the way you eliminate the nonsense and get down to business, I also feel valued as a teacher because I feel like you put yourself at our level and can relate to the obstacles or struggles we go through."

> "Sometimes during our PLCs it seems as if we are just talking about numbers and filling out the PLC form. It would be helpful if we could spend some of that time actually planning effective instruction for our students."

> "Your positivity forces us to reflect on our teaching, to think about our students and how we can push them to their full potential."

means no time to cause learning" (p. 16). If Tucker would have acted upon this belief, he never would have taken the time to ask for teacher feedback and to "cause learning" for himself as an instructional leader.

FEEDBACK AND SUSTAINABILITY

Nicol and MacFarlane-Dick (2006) posit seven principles of good feedback practices, two of which are of key significance to sustainable feedback. The first principle is the feedback must facilitate the development of self-assessment and reflection in learning for the leader. And second, the feedback must encourage leader and peer dialogue about learning. These critical notions of feedback underscore the important role that a leaders' direct supervisor plays in supporting school leaders professional growth and development by helping them utilize the feedback processes stemming from self-monitoring their own practices at increasingly higher levels. To highlight the importance and the impact of a leader's development of self-regulative capacities let's look at an example from Maplewood Elementary in Broward County School District, Fort Lauderdale, Florida.

Maplewood Elementary School

Principal Sherry Bees developed her Deliberate Practice Plan (leadership growth plan) with a student-achievement focus on increasing writing proficiency and a leadership focus on increasing the amount and kind of feedback her teachers were receiving on the implementation of a writing process entitled *Ratiocination*. Her hypothesis was that if she increased the fidelity of implementation of Ratiocination by providing immediate and specific feedback to her teachers, then student achievement would increase. Monthly, Bees charted this data (see Figure 8.5) which provided information on the three feedback questions not only to her but to her staff: (1) *Where are we going as a staff?* (2) *How are we and our students going?* and (3) *Where do we go next?* In addition to individual teacher feedback, she also prepared a weekly newsletter with embedded videos based on her observations for areas of needs and/or celebrations.

Throughout the entire year, Mrs. Bees had a laser-like focus on writing and the use of effective feedback practices. She continually reflected upon the feedback she was receiving from her teachers and students to learn from her actions and to modify her own leadership practices. She also spent time with her assistant principal, who had a very similar professional growth plan, to analyze the data and to co-construct next steps for their faculty. At the end of the year, Sherry was asked by her director to share her thinking, her learning, and her process with her elementary principal colleagues. As the year ended and Sherry reflected back on this process (personal communication, May 18, 2014), she mused, "This process was NOT easy but it was worth it!! It helped me become more focused which then allowed me to become a focused leader with a deliberate focus!!"

The development of self-regulation feedback is powerful and can have a significant impact on lifelong learning. As Professor Hattie (2012b) noted, "We all stand to benefit from knowing when to seek feedback, how to seek it, and what to do with it when we get it" (p. 23).

Figure 8.5   Impact of Ratiocination on Student Writing Proficiency, 2013–2014

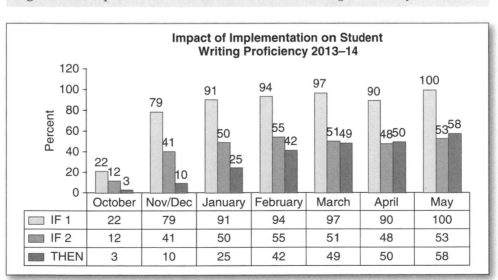

SUMMARY

When it comes to impacting student learning, we know that feedback at an effect size of 0.75 is one of the most powerful leadership practices and capabilities that a leader needs to develop. In our evaluation framework, feedback is an essential theory of practice that weaves its way through all five elements. Feedback practices require the leader to be able to continually consider and answer three important questions: *Where are we going as a staff? How are our staff and students going?* and *Where do we/I go next?* Feedback in our model addresses the importance of information to learning for school leaders, the method in which feedback is given and obtained between the participants within the evaluation cycle to promote active information processing and application, and the impact that feedback has on the participants that lead to improved leadership practices.

Deliberate Practice in Theory

9

At times, learning is not fun. Rather, it is simply hard work, consisting of deliberate practice, which we define as part of a regimen of effortful strategies designed to optimize improved professional and/or personal practice. This is not a new concept: At the close of the 19th century, Bryan and Harter (1899), for example, claimed that it took ten years to become an expert, and, in the next century, Simon and Chase (1973) found that chess masters needed to acquire some 50,000 chunks or patterns to have a chance of becoming experts. Similar to Simon and Chase, Ericsson (2000) found that the critical difference between expert musicians in terms of the attained level of solo performance was related to the amount of time spent in solitary practice during one's musical development, which totalled around 10,000 hours by the age 20 years for the best experts, a notion that Malcolm Gladwell (2008) popularized in his book *Outliers: The Story of Success*. Each of these authors and researchers underscored the fact that expertise occurs only with major investments of time.

THE PURPOSE OF THIS CHAPTER

This chapter builds on the thinking of these authors as well as on our own thinking and work with central office and school leaders across the nation in an effort to provoke leaders to consider and to change their actions when it comes to constructing and then implementing a proficient leadership growth plan. Hence, this chapter is entitled *Deliberate Practice in Theory*. The purpose of this chapter is to describe the theoretical leadership strategies underlying effective improvement planning before moving to the next chapter, in which we describe how these improvement theories practically play themselves out by showcasing the practices of real leaders in real school settings.

We have purposefully elected to use the term *deliberate practice* not only as the title to this chapter but also as the title to our leadership growth plan as the phrase signals for leaders that practice leads to competence. In the next several sections of this chapter, we walk you through the structural design of a school leader's professional growth plan, or Deliberate Practice Plan—a plan focusing on the critical elements of performance that need to be improved as part of the summative leadership performance evaluation process—and provide examples of how a fictional school leader, Nick Smith, might think his way through each of these critical elements.

SUPPORTING STATE IMPLEMENTATION EFFORTS

During our work to provide technical assistance support to school districts and leaders across the United States as they endeavor to implement state-mandated principal-evaluation models (including personal leadership improvement plans), we are routinely asked such questions as

- How does the concept of Deliberate Practice connect to the leadership evaluation process?
- How do we measure the impact of leadership practices?
- How do we use the "cause" data (e.g., measures of leadership practice) to make just-in-time adjustments to leadership practices?
- How do we monitor the implementation of the Deliberate Practice efforts of principals and make certain that they are receiving "just in time, just for them, just for where they are in their learning process, and just what they need to move forward" (Hattie, 2012b, p. 20) feedback?

Questions such as these prompted us to think more deeply about our own concept of Deliberate Practice within our instructional leadership ability framework. Consequently, our goal within this chapter is to expose our thinking and learning about Deliberate Practice to our readers in an effort to help them think more deeply about how our thinking compares to their own and ultimately how they might want to enhance their leadership actions relative to the task of creating and implementing a professional growth plan for themselves. By creating and implementing a Deliberate Practice Plan, school leaders demonstrate a focus on learning by measuring the impact of their leadership practices on student achievement. A sample of our suggested Deliberate Practice Plan Template is reflected in Figure 9.1.

DELIBERATE PRACTICE DEFINED

In all fields of human endeavor—from the arts (e.g., music, painting, writing), to sports (e.g., swimming, running, golf), to games (e.g., bridge, chess)—great performers of all stripes almost always commit

Figure 9.1   Deliberate Practice Plan (DPP) Template

Deliberate Practice Plan (DPP) Template			
School Leader's Name and Position:			
Evaluator's Name and Position:			
Target for School Year:		Date Target Approved:	
School Leader's Signature:			
Evaluator's Signature:			
Prioritized Schoolwide Problem-of-Practice			
SMART+ER Goal *(Drawn from your school improvement planning analysis linked to the problem-of-practice)*			
High-Impact Leadership Practices *(What might be 1-2 high-impact practices that could leverage goal attainment?)*			
Theory-of-Action: (What is your hypothesis e.g., "If we…, then we will…"?)			
Leadership Strategy-in-Action	Student Results *(Formative Assessment)*	Qualitative Benefits	Sources of Data to Monitor
Task Analysis *(What are some key things you anticipate you will need to do to ensure success?)*			
1.			
2.			
3.			

themselves to continually improving their performance through deliberate practice. As Colvin noted, this unrelenting desire for constant improvement requires such individuals to identify certain "sharply defined elements of [their] performance that need to be improved, and then work intently on [improving] them" (Colvin, 2008, p. 68). Colvin (2008) went on to say that a hallmark of great performers is that they "isolate remarkably specific aspects of what they do and focus on just those things until they are improved; then it's on to the next aspect" (p. 68). Another way of saying this is that learning, regardless of who is doing the learning, is most effective when the individual purposefully engages in deliberate practice that includes active monitoring of one's learning experiences compared with some established goal or standard of practice. More importantly, learning advances only as a result of monitoring one's progress toward a goal and using the feedback about one's progress in order to know what next steps to achieve the goal or standard (i.e., the desired state).

So how might school leaders set about the process of isolating remarkably specific aspects of what they do in order to focus on the most critical aspects of their role until they are improved so that their performance over time constantly improves? In order to reveal the thinking that a leader would pursue as he or she works through each of the steps related to developing and implementing an individual improvement plan, we will use a fictitious principal, Nick Smith, and his fictitious school, Marsh Middle School. However, prior to answering the question that we have just posed, a basic understanding of the architecture of the Deliberate Practice Plan Template is in order.

STRUCTURAL DESIGN OF A DELIBERATE PRACTICE PLAN

As with most planning documents, which rely upon a unique structural design that connects individual components of an improvement plan to one another in order to make a coherent whole, the structural design of the Deliberate Practice Plan Template contains nine key elements (as illustrated in Figure 9.2): (1) a Prioritized Schoolwide Problem-of-Practice, (2) the leader's SMART+ER Goal, (3) High-Impact Leadership Practices, (4) the Theory-of-Action Statement, (5) the Leadership Strategy-in-Action Statement, (6) the Student Results Statement, (7) Qualitative Benefits, (8) the Sources of Data to Monitor, and (9) the leader's Task Analysis of essential next steps to implementing the leadership strategy. A brief description of each of the nine key components and how our fictitious leader might think through each of these components based on both personal and organizational needs follows.

Component 1: Prioritized Schoolwide Problem-of-Practice

We believe that the structural design of the leader's professional growth plan must begin with a "problem-of-practice statement." The problem-of-practice statement is the foundational element of the leader's improvement plan for two reasons. First, it helps to focus the attention of the leader on a critical aspect of organizational development. That is, of all

Figure 9.2   Nine Key Elements Within the Deliberate Practice Plan Template

Deliberate Practice Plan (DPP) Template			
School Leader's Name and Position:			
Evaluator's Name and Position:			
Target for School Year:		Date Target Approved:	
School Leader's Signature:			
Evaluator's Signature:			

1 Prioritized Schoolwide Problem-of-Practice

2 SMART+ER Goal (Drawn from your school improvement planning analysis linked to the problem-of-practice)

3 High-Impact Leadership Practices *(What might be 1-2 high-impact practices that could leverage goal attainment?)*

4 Theory-of-Action: *(What is your hypothesis; e.g., "If we…, then we will…"?)*

5 Leadership Strategy-in-Action	**6** Student Results *(Formative Assessment)*	**7** Qualitative Benefits	**8** Sources of Data to Monitor

9 Task Analysis *(What are some key things you anticipate you will need to do to ensure success?)*

1.
2.
3.

of the demands on the leader's time and all of the things competing for his or her attention within the school, what central issue will be the target of his or her focus? Second, it also ensures that the leadership improvement effort will be an aligned action that benefits both the leader (by helping him or her to improve leadership practices) and the organization (by maintaining a focus on strategic targets, which are a priority for all within the system). Thus, a well-constructed problem-of-practice statement ensures that the leader's Deliberate Practice Plan will fulfill dual purposes within the organization (Smith, Brofft, Law, & Smith, 2012). A "proficient" problem-of-practice statement:

- Concentrates on learning (both for students as well as for adults);
- Focuses on classroom instruction (i.e., the actual interactions between teachers, students, and content in the classroom) or on leadership practices (i.e., how and where leaders use their influence, their learning, and their relationships with staff to positively impact the core business of teaching and learning and the operation of the organization);
- Is directly observable and measurable;
- Is actionable (i.e., is within the school's, department's, or district's direct control and influence and can be improved in real time);
- Links to a broader strategy of improvement (i.e., school, department, system); and,
- Reflects a high-leverage strategy (i.e., if acted upon, it would lead to lasting, significant improvement)

So, let's introduce our fictional principal Nick Smith and his work at Marsh Middle School to help bring to life how he thinks through each of these nine components, beginning with Component 1.

As a result of a comprehensive needs analysis that was conducted by the Marsh Middle School staff as part of their school improvement planning process, the staff collectively determined that a focus on writing would represent one of the school's highest priorities. Consequently, they formulated the following problem-of-practice statement:

Our ISTEP+ [statewide student assessment system] data reveal significant gaps in student writing achievement between our Hispanic students and our White students. In particular, students did not score well on the Writing Process component of the assessment. We may not be providing these students with enough practice with prewriting, drafting, editing, and revising relative to our expectation that they write clear, coherent, and focused expository/narrative prose.

Notice that the staff did not attempt to offer possible solutions during this first critical step; rather they worked hard to stay focused on only the problem in student learning and the potential related problems contributing to poor student performance as a result of their adult practices or the absence of practice. Consequently, Nick captured Marsh's Problem-of-Practice statement and placed it into the space immediately below that first element, which can be seen in Figure 9.3.

Component 2: The Leader's SMART+ER Goal

Just like the problem-of-practice statement, the leader's *SMART+ER* Goal should be drawn directly from the school's School Improvement Plan. The

Figure 9.3 Prioritized Schoolwide Problem-of-Practice Statement

Deliberate Practice Plan (DPP) Template	
School Leader's Name and Position:	Nick Smith, Principal, Marsh Middle School
Evaluator's Name and Position:	Dr. Julie Hellman, Director of School Improvement and Accountability
Target for School Year:	2016-17	Date Target Approved:	August 1, 2016
School Leader's Signature:	Nick Smith
Evaluator's Signature:	Julie R. Hellman

Prioritized Schoolwide Problem-of-Practice
Our ISTEP+ data reveal significant gaps in student writing achievement between our Hispanic students and our White students. In particular, students did not score well on the Writing Process component of the assessment. We may not be providing these students with enough practice with prewriting, drafting, editing, and revising relative to our expectation that they write clear, coherent, and focused expository/narrative prose.

fact that the first two elements within the Deliberate Practice Plan come from the school's continuous improvement process firmly weds the leader's individual work to perfect his or her practice with the organization's desire to continually improve. We assume that the reader is familiar with the well-used term *SMART Goal,* which generally refers to goal statements that are specific, measurable, achievable, relevant, and time-bound. It is important to note, however, that our use of the term *SMART+ER Goal* comes from our work with Cognition Education (an independent education consultancy based in New Zealand). Cognition Education has the sole proprietary rights to deliver Professor John Hattie's ground-breaking research (2009; 2012a) that is reflected in his book *Visible Learning: A Synthesis of Over 800 Meta-Analyses Relating to Achievement.*

In this case, the modified term *SMART+ER* refers to goals that are specific, measurable, ambitious (note the change from achievable), relevant, and time-bound in addition to being evaluated and re-evaluated over the course of the year. For example, given that the staff at Nick's school had identified expository writing as the schoolwide problem-of-practice (Deliberate Practice Element 1), they therefore crafted the following SMART+ER Goal as part of the school's focus on writing within their school improvement process: *"70% of our eighth-grade students (Hispanic) will meet the DOE writing criteria in Grades 6–8 and will attain Level 3.5 or above by June 2017 with monthly reevaluation of student writing."* Nick simply cut and pasted the school's SMART+ER Goal into the space below Component 2 as shown in Figure 9.4.

Figure 9.4   Marsh Middle School's SMART+ER Goal Statement

Deliberate Practice Plan (DPP) Template	
School Leader's Name and Position:	Nick Smith, Principal, Marsh Middle School
Evaluator's Name and Position:	Dr. Julie Hellman, Director of School Improvement and Accountability
Target for School Year: 2016-17 SR	Date Target Approved: August 1, 2016
School Leader's Signature: Nick Smith	
Evaluator's Signature: Julie R. Hellman	
Prioritized Schoolwide Problem-of-Practice	
Our ISTEP+ data reveal significant gaps in student writing achievement between our Hispanic students and our White students. In particular, students did not score well on the Writing Process component of the assessment. We may not be providing these students with enough practice with prewriting, drafting, editing, and revising relative to our expectation that they write clear, coherent, and focused expository prose.	
SMART+ER Goal *(Drawn from your school improvement planning analysis linked to the problem-of-practice)*	
70% of our eighth-grade students (Hispanic) will meet the DOE writing criteria in Grades 6–8 and will attain Level 3.5 or above by June 2017 with monthly reevaluation of student writing.	

Component 3: High-Impact Leadership Practices

Now that Nick has "narrowed" and "aligned" his Deliberate Practice Plan to a target that is worthy of a significant investment of his time and energy and supportive of one of his school's key areas of improvement, he turns his attention to identifying one or two high-impact leadership practices that are consistent with the research and that, when implemented well, will help him to leverage the attainment of his SMART+ER Goal. The process of thinking about which highly specific aspects of Nick's personal performance on which to focus his improvement efforts first requires self-feedback about his past performance prior to securing feedback from other sources (i.e., Nick's supervisor Dr. Hellman or his staff and/or Nick's peers).

In other words, Nick begins by reflecting on the results of the prior year's summative evaluation and the recommendations provided by his supervisor, Dr. Hellman. He notes that Dr. Hellman had identified a lack of personal involvement in the learning and professional development of his teachers with the prior year's initiatives. Her recommendation for next steps for Nick included, among other things, that Nick should

*Design more opportunities for him to personally join in teachers' profes-
sional discussions about improvement efforts because with this participation comes a greater understanding of the concepts and the vocabulary
associated with teachers' new shared learning about the respective initiative. More importantly, effective leadership of teacher professional learning involves using evidence about student learning to inform decisions
about what professional learning is needed, whether it is working, who it
is working for, and when it should end.*

Nick also reflects on an article he recently read that seemed to support
Dr. Hellman's suggestion about leaders being personally involved in the
professional development of their teachers. The article, entitled *The Impact
of Leadership on Student Outcomes: An Analysis of the Differential Effects of
Leadership Types,* concluded, "the more leaders focus their relationships,
their work, and their learning on the core business of teaching and learning, the greater their influence on student outcomes" (Robinson et al.,
2008, p. 636). Nick recognizes that inserting himself more closely in the
day-to-day work of teachers is essential.

In an effort to really triangulate on this issue, Nick decides to conduct
a quick survey of his staff to get their perceptions regarding his involvement in the improvement process. Nick thinks that several of the questions
asked within the Wallace Foundation-funded study entitled *Learning from
Leadership: Investigating the Links to Improved Student Learning* (Wahlstrom,
Louis, Leithwood, & Anderson, 2010, p. 82) might be good questions to ask
of his teachers. In particular, Nick likes the following questions (which he
modifies to fit his particular context):

- *How often in the prior school year did your principal discuss instructional
  issues with you?*
- *How often in the prior school year did your principal encourage collaborative work among staff?*
- *How often in the prior school year did your principal provide or locate
  resources to help staff improve their teaching?*
- *How often in the prior school year did your principal observe your classroom instruction?*
- *How often in the prior school year did your principal encourage data use in
  planning for individual student needs?*
- *How often in the prior school year did your principal attend teacher planning meetings?*
- *How often in the prior school year did your principal give you specific ideas
  for how to improve your instruction?*

The information from the survey is consistent with the information
provided by Dr. Hellman and the article by Robinson et al. (2008). On the
basis of these three sources of feedback, Nick determines that as the

school begins to focus this year on improving student achievement in the area of expository/narrative writing, he will develop a few key strategies that will cause him to routinely interact with his teachers as they work to implement the professional development around prewriting, drafting, editing, and revising. Nick and the teachers will use the information from the survey to support just-in-time professional development and adjustments in teaching and leadership actions. Nick is now able to complete the third element within the Deliberate Practice Plan, which is reflected in Figure 9.5.

Next, Nick must address at least three challenges. First, he must be clear as to what exactly he is expected to know and what he should be able to do in order to perform at the "Proficient" or higher performance level(s)

Figure 9.5   Nick's High-Impact Leadership Practices

Deliberate Practice Plan (DPP) Template			
School Leader's Name and Position:	Nick Smith, Principal, Marsh Middle School		
Evaluator's Name and Position:	Dr. Julie Hellman, Director of School Improvement and Accountability		
Target for School Year:	2016-2017 SR	Date Target Approved:	August 1, 2016
School Leader's Signature:	Nick Smith		
Evaluator's Signature:	Julie R. Hellman		
Prioritized Schoolwide Problem-of-Practice			
Our ISTEP+ data reveal significant gaps in student writing achievement between our Hispanic students and our White students. In particular, students did not score well on the Writing Process component of the assessment. We may not be providing these students with enough practice with prewriting, drafting, editing, and revising relative to our expectation that they write clear, coherent, and focused expository prose.			
SMART+ER Goal *(Drawn from your school improvement planning analysis linked to the problem-of-practice)*			
70% of our eighth-grade students (Hispanic) will meet the DOE writing criteria in Grades 6–8 and will attain Level 3.5 or above by June 2017 with monthly reevaluation of student writing.			
High-Impact Leadership Practices *(What might be 1 or 2 high-impact practices that could leverage goal attainment?)*			
Focus specifically on the following leadership practices relative to improving expository/ narrative student writing: • Planning, coordinating, and evaluating teaching and the curriculum • Promoting and participating in teacher learning and development			

for each of the high-impact leadership practices. Second, Nick must determine the areas of knowledge and the skills with which he already feels competent so that he can identify which areas of knowledge and which skills will constitute new learning and therefore will require professional development support. Last, he must figure out how he might apply the knowledge and skills reflected in the one or two high-impact leadership practices (e.g., specific leadership actions) to help his staff implement the "writing strategies" that they learn within their professional development offerings and accomplish the stated writing objective within his school improvement plan.

As stated above, once Nick has identified the knowledge and skills that he will be required to demonstrate in order to be "Proficient," he must determine his current areas of proficiency in order to identify which areas will require additional training in the form of professional development. The first thing Nick will want to do is to consult the evaluation rubrics (as these two high-impact leadership practices are two of five performance elements that make up the instructional leadership ability framework) and the descriptions for "Proficient" and higher practice along with Dr. Hellman's comments. If Nick has questions about the descriptions or would like a more detailed description of these practices, he might want to get a copy of Viviane Robinson's book entitled *Student-Centered Leadership* (Robinson, 2011) for more information. Furthermore, while he has a superficial understanding of effective feedback (an essential leadership function associated with the first high-impact leadership practice) and "cause" and "effect" data, he may determine that he will need some additional support in these areas. In that case, he might want to participate in one of the district's professional development offerings that address the issues of feedback and cause and effect data. Alternatively, he might want to secure a copy of John Hattie's book entitled *Visible Learning for Teachers* (2012a) or Hattie and Timperley's article entitled "The Power of Feedback" (2007) to read about these concepts and work to build them into his leadership practices.

Component 4: Theory-of-Action Statement

Having established a clear understanding of what he needs to know and be able to do to in order to demonstrate "Proficient" and higher performance in these two high-impact leadership practices, Nick must formulate a theory-of-action statement that will cause him to use the identified leadership practices (apply the knowledge) in an action-oriented manner with his staff that supports their targeted area of writing. As we described in *The Reflective Leader*,

> When, as leaders, you interact with others, you tend to design or plan your behavior and retain theories for doing so. These theories-of-action comprise the values, strategies, and underlying

assumptions that inform our patterns of interpersonal behavior. Theories-of-action operate at two levels: There are espoused theories that we use to explain or justify our behavior. And, there are theories-in-action, which are implicit in our patterns of behavior with others. In other words, there are both intended theories and enacted theories. Leaders must construct explicit theories-of-action and assess those theories against the realities of their work. (Smith et al., 2012, p. 108)

Stephen Covey (1994) helps us to think about these concepts in this way: our *intended theories* represent the "blueprint before the construction; the mental before the physical creation" (p. 111), and our *enacted theories* signify our physical creation—our actions. For improvement planning purposes, constructing an explicit theory-of-action asks the leader to begin the improvement planning process with the end in mind. This statement is almost always associated with a critical professional development offering. Let's say, for instance, that Nick's school improvement team has determined that they will tap into one of the district's professional development offerings in writing to build faculty capacity in teaching writing across content and grade levels—a key instructional shift that supports the Common Core State Standards. Specifically, they will provide the Marsh staff with professional development in differentiated writing instruction. Consequently, the theory-of-action statement will be about this professional development offering.

Given Nick's new understanding of successful implementation practices and his knowledge that teachers are key in implementing any change, he has been reminded that effective leadership is necessary for schools to experience successful change. In particular, Nick understands that successful leaders need to develop a culture of readiness for change, promote the vision, provide the necessary resources, ensure the availability of professional development, maintain checks on progress, and provide the ongoing assistance necessary for change to occur smoothly (Hall & Hord, 2011).

Consequently, Nick crafts the theory-of-action statement shown in Figure 9.6. Notice that the statement is expressed using an "If/Then" format as it reflects a theory or hunch as to what Nick is hypothesizing will happen. Simply put, the statement reflects the relationship between what he is planning on doing and the intended impact of those practices on student achievement (in a targeted area).

Component 5: Leadership Strategy-in-Action Statement

Next, Nick must translate the knowledge and skills reflected in the two high-impact leadership practices he identified into one or two specific and measurable leadership strategies. These one to two leadership

Figure 9.6   Nick's Theory-of-Practice Statement

Deliberate Practice Plan (DPP) Template			
School Leader's Name and Position:	Nick Smith, Principal, Marsh Middle School		
Evaluator's Name and Position:	Dr. Julie Hellman, Director of School Improvement and Accountability		
Target for School Year:	2016–2017 SR	Date Target Approved:	August 1, 2016
School Leader's Signature:	Nick Smith		
Evaluator's Signature:	Julie R. Hellman		
Prioritized Schoolwide Problem-of-Practice			
Our ISTEP+ data reveal significant gaps in student writing achievement between our Hispanic students and our White students. In particular, students did not score well on the Writing Process component of the assessment. We may not be providing these students with enough practice with prewriting, drafting, editing, and revising relative to our expectation that they write clear, coherent, and focused expository prose.			
SMART+ER Goal (Drawn from your school improvement planning analysis linked to the problem-of-practice)			
70% of our eighth-grade students (Hispanic) will meet the DOE writing criteria in Grades 6–8 and will attain Level 3.5 or above by June 2017 with monthly reevaluation of student writing.			
High-impact Leadership Practices (What might be 1 or 2 high-impact practices that could leverage goal attainment?)			
Focus specifically on the following leadership practices relative to improving expository/ narrative student writing: • Planning, coordinating, and evaluating teaching and the curriculum • Promoting and participating in teacher learning and development			
Theory-of-Action: (What is your hypothesis; e.g., "If we…, then we will…"?)			
If we implement differentiated writing instruction, then student writing performance will improve.			

strategies become the "Action Plan" that he will implement, monitor, and measure against improvements in student achievement (e.g., writing). Prior to offering examples of strategies, it is important to define what we mean by the phrase *leadership strategy*. A leadership strategy is: *observable,* subject to frequent public testing, and measurable (e.g., quantifiable, able to be gauged); an *obvious* translation (i.e., paraphrase) of the high-impact leadership practices; constructed with *formative language* (e.g., "increase the percentage of," "reduce the percentage of," "increase the amount or number of," etc.) as such strategies are intended to be "dipstick" measures used over time rather than goal statements; and *time-bound* (i.e., the strategy should indicate how often the public testing will occur). An illustration of a leadership strategy that Nick might develop would look something like the statement in the first column in Figure 9.7.

It is important to note that this illustrative example of a leadership strategy-in-action is observable as the instructional practice is subject to frequent (monthly) public testing (securing from teachers, by means of observation and a self-assessment rubric, the degree to which they are implementing differentiated writing instruction) and measurable (for example, if there are 30 faculty members on Nick's staff, the monthly schoolwide measurement for any one month would be the percentage of Nick's faculty, say 66% [20 of 30], who rate themselves at the "Proficient" or higher level of the rubric). Next, the strategy requires Nick to monitor faculty proficiency or effectiveness (implementation of differentiated instruction) and evaluate which staff are implementing the instruction at the "Proficient" or higher level of a rubric. Because the leadership strategy indicates that monthly increases in faculty proficiency should occur, Nick must not only give timely and actionable feedback to teachers about the differentiated writing instruction he is observing them use, he also must secure from his teachers their self-assessment of the degree to which they believe they are implementing the same writing practices so that he can use these data to support the improvement of his teachers' writing instruction.

Figure 9.7   Sample Leadership Strategy-in-Action Statement

Leadership Strategy-in-Action	Student Results (Formative Assessment)	Qualitative Benefits	Sources of Data to Monitor
• Increase the percentage of faculty implementing differentiated writing instruction at the "Proficient" or higher level based on both direct observation and teacher self-assessment monthly using a locally developed rubric			

Component 6: Student Results Statement

This leadership strategy statement, paired with the school improvement plan SMART+ER Goal of improving student achievement in writing, establishes a hypothesis that begs to be tested. For instance, if Nick and his teachers demonstrate monthly increases in faculty who are implementing the differentiated writing instruction at a "Proficient" level (or higher) according to a locally developed rubric, as described in this strategy statement, then they would expect to see similar increases in the percentage of students scoring at the "Proficient" (or higher) level of a locally developed writing assessment according to a site-developed rubric. A sample Student Results Statement is shown in the second column from the left in Figure 9.8.

Figure 9.8   Sample Student Results Statement

Leadership Strategy-in-Action	Student Results (Formative Assessment)	Qualitative Benefits	Sources of Data to Monitor
• Increase the percentage of faculty implementing differentiated writing instruction at the "Proficient" or higher level based on both direct observation and teacher self-assessment monthly using a locally developed rubric	• Increase the percentage of students scoring at the "Proficient" or higher level on a monthly writing assessment using a locally developed rubric		

Component 7: The Qualitative Benefits of Action Research

As a result of implementing this leadership strategy, several important "Qualitative Benefits" would evidence themselves (see Figure 9.9). First, Nick, along with his faculty, would become keenly aware of the barriers to proficient student writing. Second, they would develop an awareness of the instructional practices that appear to most help them overcome those barriers as well as those do not have a positive relationship to improvements in student writing. Third, Nick would learn whether or not his selected leadership strategy was having the desired impact. These *benefits* can be summarized into the category "Qualitative Benefits" as shown in the third column from the left in Figure 9.9.

Figure 9.9   Sample Qualitative Benefits Statements

Leadership Strategy-in-Action	Student Results (Formative Assessment)	Qualitative Benefits	Sources of Data to Monitor
• Increase the percentage of faculty implementing differentiated writing instruction at the "Proficient" or higher level based on both direct observation and teacher self-assessment monthly using a locally developed rubric	• Increase the percentage of students scoring at the "Proficient" or higher level on a monthly writing assessment using a locally developed rubric	• Become keenly aware of the barriers to proficient student writing • Develop an awareness of the instructional practices that appear to most help students overcome those barriers as well as those practices that don't have a positive relationship to improvements in student writing • Determine whether or not the selected leadership strategy-in-action is having the desired impact	

Component 8: Determining Sources of Data to Monitor

Next, Nick needs to identify the "Sources of Data to Monitor" so he can determine the impact of his leadership strategy-in-action on student writing. Put plainly, Nick must be clear as to what data he will monitor each month in order to keep a finger on the pulse of his action plan (see column four from the left in Figure 9.10). The results of Nick's monthly monitoring will be used to adjust his leadership practices (i.e., how best to support teachers' deeper implementation of effective writing strategies).

Component 9: Task Analysis of Key Steps

Last, Nick will want to identify the key steps that he will need to take to ensure success. The aim of this last step in the development of his Deliberate Practice Plan is to perform a task analysis of the plan. Put another way, Nick will need to identify all of those things he (they) must

Figure 9.10   Sample Sources of Data to Monitor Statements

Leadership Strategy-in-Action	Student Results (Formative Assessment)	Qualitative Benefits	Sources of Data to Monitor
• Increase the percentage of faculty implementing differentiated writing instruction at the "Proficient" or higher level based on both direct observation and teacher self-assessment monthly using a locally developed rubric	• Increase the percentage of students scoring at the "Proficient" or higher level on a monthly writing assessment using a locally developed rubric	• Become keenly aware of the barriers to proficient student writing • Develop an awareness of the instructional practices that appear to most help students overcome those barriers as well as those practices that don't have a positive relationship to improvements in student writing • Determine whether the selected leadership strategy-in-action is having the desired impact or not	• Monthly rubric results of teachers' self-assessment • Monthly rubric results of the school leader's observed assessment • Monthly rubric results from student writing performance

do in order to implement the strategy-in-action. The critical function of this step is to answer the question, "What are all of those important tasks I/we must complete in order to implement the strategy-in-action and achieve the desired results?" These are the items that typically occupy most improvement plans; they are typically not measurable strategies beyond a binary measure (did we do them or not?) because they represent actions that must happen but that, once completed, are finished. A sample (partial) task analysis is shown in Figure 9.11.

Nick's fully completed Deliberate Practice Plan, which combines all of the information presented in Figures 9.3–9.11, is depicted in Figure 9.12.

The Deliberate Practice Plan depicted in Figure 9.12 in its simple, straightforward, uncluttered form expresses Nick's structured goal-setting process that describes the goals on which Nick will concentrate and to

Figure 9.11   Sample (Partial) Task Analysis Statements

Task Analysis (What are some key things you anticipate you will need to do to ensure success?)
1. Schedule and conduct a differentiated writing strategies workshop for faculty
2. As a result of the professional development on differentiated writing, build a differentiated writing rubric that clearly describes teacher instructional practices in four performance areas (i.e., Exemplary, Proficient, Progressing, and Not Meeting Standards)
3. Construct a student writing rubric
4. Conduct student writing rubric calibration trainings
5. Translate student writing rubrics into student-friendly language

Figure 9.12   Nick's Completed Deliberate Practice Plan

Deliberate Practice Plan (DPP)		
School Leader's Name and Position:	Nick Smith, Principal, Marsh Middle School	
Evaluator's Name and Position:	Dr. Julie Hellman, Director of School Improvement and Accountability	
Target for School Year:	2016–2017 SY	Date Target Approved: August 1, 2016
School Leader's Signature:	Nick Smith	
Evaluator's Signature:	Julie R. Hellman	
Prioritized Schoolwide Problem-of-Practice		
Our ISTEP+ data reveal significant gaps in student writing achievement between our Hispanic students and our White students. In particular, students did not score well on the Writing Process component of the assessment. We may not be providing these students with enough practice with prewriting, drafting, editing, and revising relative to our expectation that they write clear, coherent, and focused expository prose.		
SMART+ER Goal *(Drawn from your school improvement planning analysis linked to the problem-of-practice)*		
70% of our eighth-grade students (Hispanic) will meet the DOE writing criteria in Grades 6–8 and will attain Level 3.5 or above by June 2017 with monthly reevaluation of student writing.		
High-Impact Leadership Practices *(What might be 1 or 2 high-impact practices that could leverage goal attainment?)*		
Focus specifically on the following leadership practices relative to improving expository/narrative student writing: • Planning, coordinating, and evaluating teaching and the curriculum • Promoting and participating in teacher learning and development		

Theory of Action: *(What is your hypothesis; e.g.,"It we…, then we will…"?)*			
If we implement differentiated writing instruction, then student writing performance will improve.			
Leadership Strategy-in-Action	Student Results *(Formative Assessment)*	Qualitative Benefits	Sources of Data to Monitor
Increase the percent of faculty implementing differentiated writing instruction at the "Proficient" or higher level based on both direct observation and teacher self-assessment monthly using a locally developed rubric	Increase the percent of students scoring at the "Proficient" and higher levels on a monthly writing assessment using a locally developed rubric	• Become keenly aware of the barriers to proficient student writing • Develop an awareness of the instructional practices that appear to most help students overcome those barriers as well as those practices that don't have a positive relationship to improvements in student writing • Determine whether the selected leadership strategy-in-action is having the desired impact or not	• Monthly rubric results of teachers' self-assessment • Monthly rubric results of the school leader's observed assessment • Monthly rubric results from student writing performance
Task Analysis *(What are some key things you anticipate you will need to do to ensure success?)*			

1. Schedule and conduct a differentiated writing strategies workshop for faculty
2. As a result of the professional development on differentiated writing build a differentiated writing rubric that clearly describes teacher instructional practices in four performance areas (i.e., Exemplary, Proficient, Progressing, and Not Meeting Standards)
3. Construct a student writing rubric
4. Conduct student writing rubric calibration trainings
5. Translate student writing rubrics into student friendly language

which he will devote his prioritized attention. As such, Nick's Deliberate Practice meets the criteria that Hattie and Yates (2014) suggested are essential to this type of effort. Specifically, Hattie and Yates (2014) suggest that for deliberate practice to be deliberate practice and not simply practice for practice sake, it must be "developmental, effortful, goal-structured, and actively monitored" (p. 100).

The next chapter highlights the work of Rob Zook, principal at Concord Junior High School, James Neihof, superintendent in Shelby County Public Schools, and Dr. Ted Toomer, principal at Lyons Creek Middle School, as real-world examples of educators who have successfully implemented the concept of Deliberate Practice within their workplaces.

SUMMARY

In summary, the professional improvement plan process entitled Deliberate Practice was discussed. Each of the nine key components was described. Specifically, we emphasized the importance of leaders isolating remarkably specific aspects of their practices on which to focus until they are improved. Next, we presented the nine elements comprising the structural design of our Deliberate Practice Planning model and provided explicit examples of what each might look like through a fictional leader's perspective.

Deliberate Practice in Application

I n the last chapter, we presented for your consideration a theoretical model of a professional growth plan that we termed *Deliberate Practice*. This brief chapter is meant to be instructive and practical in nature and has two intended purposes. The first purpose, and perhaps the most important, is to hold up for everyone to review and use the excellent instructional leadership ability work of three leaders with whom we have had the great privilege to work. The second purpose is to provide—as is so often requested during our presentations—real-world illustrations of the practices we are espousing. In other words, participants routinely ask us, *"Who is implementing this practice and what are their results?"* What follows, then, is the highlighted work of three educational leaders—Mr. Rob Zook, Mr. James Neihoff, and Dr. Ted Toomer—as they illustrate for you the ways in which they applied the concept of Deliberate Practice within their school setting.

CONCORD COMMUNITY SCHOOLS

Rob Zook, principal at Concord Junior High School in Concord Community Schools, Elkhart, Indiana, demonstrates the power of engaging in deliberate practice that includes active monitoring of one's learning experiences in comparison with some established goal or standard of practice. Specifically, Rob wanted to improve student performance on the Mathematics and English/Language Arts portions of the Indiana Statewide Testing for Educational Progress Plus (ISTEP+) while decreasing absenteeism, failing grades, and student in-school and out-of-school suspensions.

Rob, along with his faculty, speculated that they could do a better job of helping students assume more ownership of their learning in such areas as grades, attendance, Acuity Assessment results (a CTB/McGraw-Hill predictive and diagnostic assessment), and behavioral issues that in the past have had a negative impact on student performance. Toward that end, teachers met one-on-one with students throughout the year to check in with them on their performance in the previously identified areas. By frequently connecting with students in this manner, teachers demonstrated that they cared for the learning of each student as a person (which sends a powerful message about purpose and priority). According to John Hattie (2009), building relationships with students is a high-impact instructional practice that helps teachers to better understand student perspectives and helps students to feel safe and cared for in their school (Bryk & Schneider, 2002). Figure 10.1 shows the deliberate practice plan that Concord Junior High School constructed in an effort to focus its improvement efforts. Although the organization of the Concord Community Schools plan contains slightly different components than the one we suggested in Figure 9.12, the overall intent remains the same.

Concord Junior High School Deliberate Practice Plan

As a result of their collective improvement efforts, the Concord Junior High Faculty exceeded their projected results in three of the four improvement categories. In other words, the percentage of students passing both Math and English/Language Arts ISTEP+ increased by 6.3%, at the same time the percentage of students receiving a failing grade in the 4th Quarter decreased by 8.7%, and the number of out-of-school suspensions alone decreased 170 in 2010–2011 to 120 in 2011–2012, representing a 30% decrease. Moreover, Concord Junior High moved from a 2011 State School Grade of "D" to a State School Grade of "A" for 2012.

PUBLIC DISPLAYS OF IMPACT

Publicly displaying the results of improvement efforts has been shown to have a powerful impact on student achievement. In his synthesis of more than 800 meta-analyses, Professor John Hattie (2009) concluded this about the value of teachers graphing data:

> When teachers were required to use data and evidence based models [to ascertain how students are achieving learning intentions they have set for students, such that they can then decide where students need to go next], effect sizes were higher than when data were evaluated by teacher judgment. In addition, when the data was graphed, effect sizes were higher than when the data was simply recorded. (p. 181)

Although as we realize Hattie's comments refer to teachers working with students in a classroom and not principals working with teachers in

Figure 10.1   Concord Junior High School's Deliberate Practice Plan

Schoolwide Problem-of-Practice: *(Abbreviated Data Analysis Narrative)*	Traditionally, our ISTEP+ data reveal that approximately 25% to 30% of Concord Junior High School students fail to demonstrate proficiency in Math and/or English/Language Arts. Of these failing students there is a prevailing trend of disengagement and non-ownership in their education. This trend has a negative effect on daily attendance rates, classroom grades, and student behavior. Staff may not be helping students take ownership for their own learning.		
Theories-of-Action: *(Hypothesis—IF/ THEN—Statements from Inquiry Process)*	If we implement a student accountability plan during CAP with intention and integrity, while administrators provide specific feedback through classroom walkthroughs, then students will take ownership and responsibility regarding aspects of their education. This engagement will have a positive impact on overall attendance rates, grades, behavior, and ISTEP+ results.		
SMART Goal Statement 1:	**By May 2012, we will see the following improvements as compared to the school year 2010–2011**		
	(1) The percentage of students proficient in both Math and E/LA ISTEP+ will increase from 61% to 66%.		
	(2) The number of students with 10 or more absences will decrease from 25.8% to 19.4%.		
	(3) The percentage of students earning a failing 4th Quarter class grade will decrease from 29.3% to 22%.		
	(4) The total number of OSS/ISS will decrease 25%.		
Leadership Implementation Strategies: *(Insert your 1–3 measurable leadership strategies).* **IF I . . .**	**Results Indicators** *(A measurable, percentage, increase in student learning results)* **THEN** *I expect to see . . .*	**Desired Benefits** *(Create descriptions of proficient teacher/ leader practices to look for. Use language from rubrics here.)*	**Sources of Data to Monitor** *(Insert what student/ adult data you will monitor)*
Increase the frequency of monitoring the effectiveness of adult actions through classroom walkthroughs	Students making academic gains as measured by ISTEP+, Acuity, and classroom grade distributions	A focus on student engagement and ownership	• Classroom walkthrough data • Quarterly acuity data • Quarterly grades • Quarterly student attendance • Staff CAP binder
Monitor the level of fidelity in which teachers implement our Student Accountability Plan	An improvement in student attendance rates and a decrease in the number of incidence resulting in OSS/ISS.	Positive relationships between teachers and students	

a school, we believe they are corollary concepts. In other words, we believe that it is a fair analogy to compare principals working with teachers in a school to teachers working with students in a classroom. Consequently, we believe when principals are required to use data and evidence-based models to ascertain how teachers are achieving established learning intentions, such that principals can then decide where teachers need to go next, effect sizes should be higher than when data are evaluated on the basis of principal judgment only. In addition, we contend that when the data are graphed, effect sizes should be higher than when the data are simply recorded. The point is that graphing the results of action research is critical and reinforces the often-cited maxim, "What gets measured gets done." This maxim simply means that regular measurement and reporting keeps you focused—because you use that information to know your impact and make decisions to improve your results.

SHELBY COUNTY PUBLIC SCHOOLS

Shelby County Public Schools in Shelbyville, Kentucky, represent a prime example of the importance of educators engaging in *public displays of impact*. Mr. James Neihof, Superintendent of Schools, implemented a districtwide Plan on a Page (POP) for each of his school leaders, what we refer to as a *Deliberate Practice Plan* in our instructional leadership framework.

In a personal conversation with us, Mr. Neihof talked about an email that he sent out to his staff regarding a phenomenon he referred to as "The Google Bump." The phrase *The Google Bump* references a practice employed by the Google company relative to how it designed its cafeteria space. Essentially, Google wanted to ensure that employees would "bump into" each other during breaks and, in doing so, share the ideas on which they were working. What Mr. Neihof was stressing with his school leaders was the importance of working together collectively as a team. Thus, when school leaders monitor, measure, display, and collectively think and talk about the most perplexing schoolwide problems of practice and the results of their implementation efforts, just like the Google Bump, they too create webs of connected conversations for people to "bump into" the continuous improvement questions and solutions that really matter for Shelby County Public Schools.

This problem-centered strategy of principal support groups, in which principals periodically present their POPs to one another, is aimed at creating a culture of mutual dependency, one in which other principals and also the Superintendent and his or her central office directors are viewed as supportive colleagues. This strategy of orchestrating group discussion of problems in instructional practice contrasts markedly with the normal culture of schools and districts, in which teachers are isolated in their classrooms and principals in their buildings. Rather, what is needed are more leaders like Mr. Neihoff who create for school leaders easy access to the organization's knowledge base, its collective brain.

Let's return to our fictional school leader Nick Smith for a moment and see how he might depict his school's collective efforts to improve student achievement as a result of leveraging a handful of "sharply defined elements" of leadership performance (see Figure 10.2). Notice that in this fictional illustration, both the percentage of teachers implementing differentiated writing instruction monthly is compared with student performance on a monthly writing assessment and scored using a common writing rubric.

Graphing adult *cause data* (what the adults, teachers, and leaders in the school do that strongly relates to improved student effects) and its impact on student *effect data* (the results of student performance in writing) is useful in several ways.

First, the graph serves as a constant reminder to school leaders of the degree to which their most important leadership practices are having an impact on their core business—teaching and learning. Second, publicly reviewing these data with faculty, perhaps during a monthly faculty meeting, is an excellent way to celebrate "short-term wins" and discuss

Figure 10.2   Sample Adult Strategy Versus Student Achievement Monitoring Graph

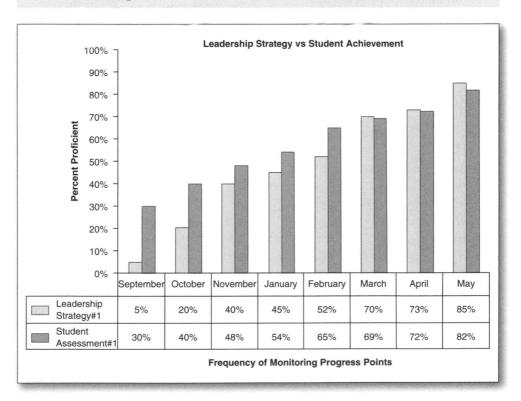

	September	October	November	January	February	March	April	May
Leadership Strategy#1	5%	20%	40%	45%	52%	70%	73%	85%
Student Assessment#1	30%	40%	48%	54%	65%	69%	72%	82%

Frequency of Monitoring Progress Points

unplanned losses (when and if the identified strategy may not be working as it was intended). Third, by graphing the relationship of adult actions to student achievement, school leaders can promote the collective efficacy of their staff. In addition, a graphic display of this nature can be used with supervisors during formative evaluation settings as they spawn numerous constructive conversations about teaching, learning, and leadership. For instance, graphs of this nature might cause either the school leader or his or her supervisor to ask such questions as

- What might be some of the "key learnings" about instructional practices, which seem to have the greatest impact on student _____ (insert the content area)? Which do not seem to have a positive impact?
- What are some of the barriers to improved student achievement in _____ (insert the content area)?
- What are some of the adjustments in leadership practice you have to make as a result of supporting teacher growth in _____ (insert the content area)?
- What else do you need in terms of knowledge and/or skills to be more effective in using this/these practices?
- What additional support might the supervisor provide the school leader based on the leader's Deliberate Practice results?
- What percentage of your staff is "Proficiently" implementing the identified high-effect size instructional practices? What support strategies are you providing staff who are not yet implementing essential instructional practices proficiently?

LYONS CREEK MIDDLE SCHOOL

Having just reviewed Nick's fictional monitoring graph in Figure 10.2, let's close this chapter with another real-world example of how important it is to collect, chart, and publicly display improvement data. Dr. Ted Toomer, principal at Lyons Creek Middle School in Broward County Public Schools, Fort Lauderdale, Florida, determined that his Deliberate Practice Plan would focus on improving students' reading scores. During the 2013–2014 school year, 62% of the Lyons Creek Middle School students were proficient in reading based on their state assessment, Florida's Comprehensive Assessment Test (FCAT). Ted's goal for the 2013–2014 School Year was 72%. In a personal conversation with us about his improvement plan, Ted indicated that,

> The instructional practice we worked on schoolwide was [improving] teacher questioning and [increasing] student discussion [in classrooms]. With a kick-start from [Dr. Smith], I presented the

questioning scale [rubric] to the faculty for their input. We modi
fied the scale to our satisfaction and began taking data. (Toomer,
personal communication, April 15, 2014).

Ted's plan was fairly straightforward. He hypothesized that student
reading scores would increase if they increased "the percent of teacher
questioning and student discussion at the 'Proficient' or higher level based
on progress monitoring assessments, direct observation, and feedback"
(Toomer, 2013, p. 1). This was a sound hypothesis for Dr. Toomer to construct given the fact that teachers in many of our classrooms across this
nation out-talk students by a 3:1 margin (Hattie & Yates, 2014). Specifically,
"about 75 percent of class time" (Hattie & Yates, 2014, p. 45) in many of our
schools is devoted to teachers talking, with as little as 5% of that time being
available to students to respond to teacher questions. Consequently, Ted
wanted to change these metrics. His progress monitoring points consisted
of monthly measures of the percentage of students scoring at the proficient
or higher level on FCAT mini-assessments compared with the percentage
of faculty questioning and engaging students in discussions at the proficient or higher level based on a locally developed instrument. The results
of their year-long improvement effort are reflected in Figure 10.3
What is immediately obvious is that Ted and the Lyons Creek Middle
School Faculty more than doubled the rate of student proficiency on their
local reading assessment from the baseline value of 32% in September 2013

Figure 10.3 Lyons Creek Middle School improvement data

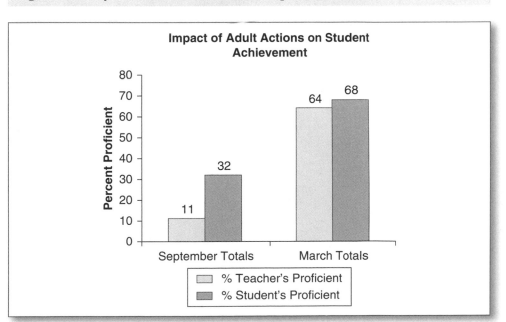

to 68% on the FCAT mini-assessment in March 2014. At the same time, faculty proficiency in teacher questioning and student discussion increased sixfold from 11% in September 2013 to 64% in March 2014. One of the most important roles of leaders, a role that Dr. Toomer is showcasing for us in this example, is to enhance the skills and knowledge of people within the organization, thereby shaping a school culture of expectations based on the proficient application of those skills and knowledge, galvanizing the various elements of the organization together in a constructive relationship with one another, and holding members accountable for their contributions to the group's results.

SUMMARY

In summary, the professional growth plan process that we presented in the previous chapter, which we termed *Deliberate Practice*, was portrayed this time in a very practical manner through the lens of three educational leaders. Specifically, we highlighted the exemplary instructional leadership work of three individuals—Mr. Rob Zook, principal at Concord Junior High School in Concord Community Schools, in Elkhart, Indiana; Mr. James Neihof, superintendent in Shelby County Public Schools, Shelbyville, Kentucky; and Dr. Ted Toomer, principal at Lyons Creek Middle School, Broward County Schools, Fort Lauderdale, Florida—as real-world examples of educators who have successfully implemented the concept of Deliberate Practice. More importantly, the work of these fine leaders serves as a model for others throughout the international educational community to apply within their organizations.

Putting It All Together

Our research suggests that the degree of implementation of initiatives, including such things as a new principal-evaluation system or a principal professional growth plan, by school leaders is a powerful variable that is often independent of the brand name of the program. Another way of saying this is that great programs that are poorly implemented have little opportunity for positive impact. Moreover, great programs that are layered on top of one another with insufficient time and attention also have little opportunity for positive impact. Consequently, we have come to learn that there is an antidote to counteracting the effects of poor implementation. The remedy to this malady is threefold: (1) identify a few (i.e., one to three) high-impact targets on which to focus your attention and resources; (2) ensure that you religiously and frequently (i.e., monthly) monitor and measure the degree to which initiatives are implemented (i.e., according to a clearly established standard of expected practice); and (3) use the results of your monitoring and measuring to make adjustments to practice to continuously improve your impact. These remedies, which are simple to say but hard to do, are research-based and constitute an essential yet often overlooked series of leadership practices.

The purpose of this final chapter is to stir your thinking about how you might approach the implementation of our instructional leadership ability framework. Toward that end, we recommend that organizations consider at least two practices. First, create and use stories, case studies, of exemplary and proficient leadership practice around the leadership evaluation criteria to take highly effective leadership practice to scale. Second, generate rubrics, word descriptions, of expected leadership practice as a way to control for human variation within the system that naturally occurs anytime individuals attempt to implement new initiatives.

THE USE OF CASE STUDIES

Case studies have been used for training programs for a long time, with a wide variety of content and formats (Connelly, Allen, & Waples, 2007). Doug Reeves (2009), in his book *Assessing Educational Leaders: Evaluating Performance for Improved Individual and Organizational Results,* suggested that organizations should be encouraged to create "realistic stories with rich descriptions of human behavior and decision-making processes . . . that portray exemplary performance" (p. 81) for each of the leadership standards that school districts have identified as defining what school leaders must know and be able to do in order to meet and/or exceed both district and school targets. These case studies, when used strategically by district leaders, help school leaders, from the most veteran to the most novice, to identify the actions that produce the desired effects. In addition, case studies of exemplary leadership performance also help leaders to visualize practices that, many times, given the isolation of leaders in their schools, will remain largely unseen by their peers. In this way, organizations "socialize its leaders into the organization (e.g., help them learn the knowledge, skills, behaviors, social values, and beliefs necessary to function effectively as members of the organization)" (Smith, Brofft, Law, & Smith, 2012, p. 131).

For example, Instructional Leadership Ability Element 4, *Leading and Participating in Teacher/Leader Learning and Development,* involves leaders being able to first and foremost be a leader of and at the same time be a participant within teachers' professional learning experiences. Additionally, leaders must identify, strategically resource, and implement high-quality collaborative opportunities that will help teachers to improve their specific instructional knowledge and skill sets in order to help all students move with success and confidence to the next educational level. Based on the description of exemplary performance in this leadership element (as defined in the rubric described in Chapter 6), a school district might create a case study such as this:

> *Six years had passed since Marek first became a principal in Pacific County. The first year went by in a blink and had been a learning experience given the unique circumstances that he faced when he moved into the role of principal at Haystack Rock High School. The previous principal of the high school had suddenly left in the middle of the year due to health issues, and Marek had been asked to serve as interim principal until the end of the year, when the job would be posted. His learning curve for those last six months of that year was huge, but Marek felt good about how he ended the school year. When his interim position was posted, he interviewed and after a lengthy process was officially named principal of Haystack Rock. Marek was now ending his first semester of his sixth year as principal and still considered himself to be on a learning curve, which was just a little less steep by this time.*

Two of Marek's favorite activities for his own leadership renewal were reading the professional research and participating in professional development. Through his reading of the research, Marek guided himself to professional resources and activities that tied directly to the needs of his school. He discovered among other things that he seemed to be more committed to and engaged in immediate application of new learning if this was the case. Marek also encouraged his colleagues to join him in these opportunities so that he could formally and informally share ideas and problems of practice that arise as a result of implementing new knowledge and skills. Besides, Marek always learned more when he could discuss practical application of learning with his peers.

This past summer, Marek had taken on an extensive school improvement plan along with other district leaders and key members of his staff as they began to implement the new Common Core State Standards. He knew that it was critical that he, along with his leadership team, work together to devise, and effectively implement, a school improvement plan that focused the collective efforts of the faculty on one to two priority targets. Marek had engaged his staff in some reflective inquiry, which helped him evaluate previous professional development opportunities to ensure that they were tightly aligned with the goals of the school and producing the desired impact on student achievement.

An important component of the Common Core State Standards, cross-content writing standards, would present a new challenge to staff, and a thoughtfully engineered implementation plan would usher in greater success. Most importantly, Marek wanted to avoid what had happened three years earlier, when the school attempted to implement Thinking Maps into teachers' classroom instruction. Unfortunately, when Marek and his teachers analyzed the cause/effect relationship at the end of the year between the Thinking Map professional development and the actual impact of these practices on student achievement, it seemed there was little to no correlation. Speculation as to why the lack of success with these instructional strategies resulted in the staff concluding that the expectations were unclear, the monitoring was too infrequent, and the data collected were not used to support ongoing teacher/leader learning. Consequently, the initiative was abandoned in the interest of the next new idea. Jumping nervously from one reform idea to the next over relatively short periods of time and implementing them in shallow ways as they had done previously would be avoided this time.

When Marek pulled together his leadership team, they held several planning sessions to examine the tie between the current student achievement data and the Common Core State Standards instructional expectations. The team found that survey data indicated that teachers were unclear about how to engage in cross-content writing that would meet the intent of the new standards. Additionally, teachers expressed confusion about what specific standards they should focus on given the number of standards cited in the new expectations. Student achievement data also indicated that students struggled in the area of nonfiction writing.

(Continued)

(Continued)

A comprehensive plan was developed to engage in ongoing professional learning in cross-content writing throughout the year. The full staff participated in a two-day Common Core State Standards workshop that walked staff through a prioritization process and allowed them to focus on key standards in a strategic manner. Marek and his leadership team also developed (with the assistance of key subject matter leaders) and implemented a cross-content writing rubric that clearly articulated for faculty the instructional writing practices that teachers were expected to use as they planned and delivered lessons. Last, the staff worked in both grade-level and cross-content teams to develop several common nonfiction-writing rubrics (i.e., argument, informative/explanatory, and narrative). Marek had received extensive training in cross-content writing and was able to lead department teams through professional development to expand their understanding of how to routinely incorporate writing into their instruction. Teachers commented later in the year about how this small-group support from Marek had made them feel more comfortable with the process.

Staff self-assessment data, gathered monthly throughout the year from teachers to monitor the implementation of cross-content writing, indicated that, each month, Marek's teachers were gaining greater insight and confidence in their implementation efforts. More importantly, the monthly feedback from staff allowed Marek and teacher leaders to adjust the professional learning support along the way. The final evaluation of the year compared the increased proficiency of teachers in implementing cross-content writing with the increased proficiency of students in producing a piece of nonfiction writing. Another aspect of the final evaluation consisted of calculating the overall effect size for a group of students between Grade 9 and Grade 10 on the statewide assessment in the area of writing. Inasmuch as the end analysis showed an overall effect size of 0.37 (almost a year's gain in writing), the calculation of individual student effect sizes revealed that the top quartile of students made more progress in writing than the bottom quartile of students. So, there were definitely some areas that could be improved upon for the following year; however, Marek was pleased with what teachers had to say about their application of this new learning to their daily practice.

Typically, the characters depicted in scenarios such as this one are either creating problems through their own actions or are being confronted with problems resulting from the behavior or actions of others. It is the problem dimension of human behavior in school leadership, however, rather than the routine duties, that should be studied, and it is this aspect toward which organizations keen on developing leadership capacity need to direct most of their attention if prospective and experienced administrators and supervisors are to be equipped with the knowledge and skills required for the 21st century. The benefit of having collective dialogue about leadership scenarios is in the convergence of meaning that results from peers' reciprocal reflection. Moreover, if the reciprocal reflection produced as a result of analysing the scenario leads you to a discussion of your own organization where people see similarities between the scenario and the context within which they work, then learning is taking place. Open discussion of this nature serves a dual purpose: it helps supervisors to better understand leadership best practices, and it helps practicing leaders to align their own styles with the culture and values of their organization.

USING RUBRICS RELIABLY

What is a rubric? Rubrics (or *scoring tools*) are a way of describing evaluation criteria (or *grading standards*) on the basis of the expected outcomes and performances of students and adults. Typically, rubrics are used in scoring or grading written assignments, performances, or oral presentations; however, they may also be used to assess any form of student or adult practice and, according to Jonsson and Svingby (2007), to enhance the reliable scoring of a performance. Similarly, each of our five Instructional Leadership Ability Rubrics consists of a set of scoring criteria (word picture descriptions of leadership behavior) and quality ratings associated with these criteria. In most rubrics, the criteria are grouped into categories so that the instructor (or supervisor in our case) and the leader being evaluated can discriminate among the categories according to level of performance. In organizational use, the rubric provides an "objective" *external standard* against which leadership performance may be compared.

Most people have difficulty in using rubrics reliably at first without some practice. The fact is, in order for an assessment tool to be used effectively, it must be used on a regular basis (more than just one or two times a year). Rubrics are most effective when you practice using them with your staff over and over again, making certain to clarify any vague terms or to quantify phrases that require further definition. For example, the word "implementation" is almost always used within principal-evaluation instruments. After all, successfully implementing a variety of initiatives is a critical leadership role. However, the word "implementation" is vague and requires one to ask such questions as, "Implementation to what degree?" Additionally, we often see the phrase "routinely monitoring" being used within leadership evaluation documents as if the phrase enjoys some universal understanding among educators. Without further clarification, one leader might interpret "routinely" to mean three or four times per year, another leader might interpret it as meaning six or seven times per year, and yet another leader might interpret it to mean twice a year. Consequently, whether you are adopting our instructional leadership ability rubrics, revising our rubrics to fit your own particular context and vernacular, or developing your own leadership rubrics, the use of rubrics requires clarification and/or revision based on feedback from your central office and school leadership staff. The best rubrics are almost always byproducts of an iterative effort. In other words, the effectiveness of a rubric description relies on co-constructing meaning between the supervisor and the leader, through feedback, so that each can make the appropriate adjustments to his or her thinking ahead of any formal or informal assessment.

Even the best leadership evaluation framework, however, cannot succeed without equally effective implementation. Thus, it is critical to the overall accuracy and reliability of the evaluation system that evaluators share a common understanding of performance expectations and rating levels. To make certain that your school district achieves overall accuracy and reliability when using our evaluation system, we recommend that districts conduct "norming sessions" during which all leaders review leadership performance criteria in the form of case studies, assign a score, and then discuss their scores and identify precisely why they assigned the score they did. Using a rubric and holding "norming sessions" help organizations achieve "inter-rater reliability."

The "norming sessions" are an essential part of an organization's efforts to establishing common understanding of leadership performance expectations. Consequently, we suggest that you meet once or twice a semester, with all supervisors of leaders being invited. During a session, you would review key leadership elements and practices (e.g., promoting and participating in teacher/leader learning, enhancing teacher effectiveness, etc.) and their related rubrics, silently evaluate a few sample case studies, and then specifically discuss individual scores with small groups. Based on our work with clients across the nation, we believe that you will find, as we have found, that these discussions are quite lively and important because you are talking about your leadership expectations for performance and your schools in a productive, focused way. What follows such a meeting is that leaders leave the "norming session" reflecting on how their own leadership practices compare with the norm. This form of informal feedback helps principals to know where they are in relationship to the learning intention (i.e., the proficient or higher practice of the element) and what next steps they need to take to move themselves closer to goal attainment.

Alternatively, we have heard of districts making use of the leadership rubrics and norming sessions during their monthly districtwide meetings with all administrators. During these routine monthly meetings, each administrator is given the same amount of time and the same scenario to review (again, you might want to select key leadership elements or theories of practice on which to focus your organizational thinking) ahead of the actual meeting. On the day of your districtwide meeting, you have your own "norming session" in small, three to six-member teams of administrators. Begin by giving the administrators copies of the specific rubrics (the leadership elements) and explain how to use them. Next, have them silently score each of the scenarios. Last, spend the rest of the allotted time discussing each of the scenarios in great depth, digging in to understand why individuals scored the leadership action at a specific performance level (i.e., what evidence they used to assign their scores). It is important that you keep referring to the rubrics that you have provided, which, of course, are a clear statement of your leadership expectations and a reflection of expected leadership practices that you are trying to replicate and take to scale across the district. There is great value in this process as school leaders quickly see some of the errors or weaknesses in their own leadership practices that require some adjustment. More importantly, by frequently engaging your school leaders in the process of assessment, you can

- Develop a clearly articulated and common understanding as to what high-quality leadership looks like in practice.
- Build a collaborative learning culture that replaces the compliance orientation that is typical of most districts with one of engagement, collaboration, and continuous learning. To be successful in facilitating student learning and the higherorder skills of analysis, inquiry, and creative problem solving, districts must develop and encourage these same skills in the leaders within the system.
- Develop and implement coherent systemwide leadership strategies that support the kinds of teaching and learning that districts want in all of their schools.

WHY DEVELOP AN IMPLEMENTATION RUBRIC?

An implementation rubric is a means of describing such things as what a proficiently developed Deliberate Practice Plan "looks like" (at both the developmental and implementation levels) when fully implemented (Hall & Hord, 2011). The following Deliberate Practice Development and Implementation Rubrics (see Figure 11.1) paints a series of "word pictures" of the school leader behaviors and practices and also describes the behaviors and practices as school leaders move from the "Not Meeting Expectations" variation toward the "Exemplary" variation.

USING AN IMPLEMENTATION RUBRIC

The Deliberate Practice implementation and development rubrics help everyone who is involved in implementing the Deliberate Practice Plan (e.g., school leaders, central office supervisors, etc.) to develop a common understanding of the learning intention; that is, it helps them to know where they are headed and to keep this end in mind. Beginning with the "end in mind" concept (Covey, 1989, p. 99), or creating the intended action prior to the enacted action, helps leaders to focus their efforts on the right work and avoid the problem of everyone doing things differently based on their idiosyncratic interpretations of what the practice looks like. Additionally, the Deliberate Practice Implementation and Development Rubrics help leaders and supervisors of leaders to figure out where they are and what they need to do in order to move toward full implementation. For example, individual school leaders as well as central office leadership can use the rubric to determine progress in developing and implementing Deliberate Practice and decide where to target specific training that will be most effective in moving school leaders toward the desired state.

School leaders should use these two documents to determine what variation (e.g., Exemplary, Proficient, etc.) within either the development or the implementation of the Deliberate Practice Plan predominates throughout the district. School leaders' reflections should be as candid as possible when determining their level of performance; this is not a rating tool but rather is a tool of self-assessment that will help school leaders determine where they are in the development and implementation process and what next steps they need to take.

As a measurement tool, central office leaders may elect to have school leaders self-assess using the Deliberate Practice Implementation Rubric monthly. By summarizing the data that they collect (e.g., the specific variations that predominate in their school leaders), central office leaders can model for their principals how to use data to inform leadership behaviors and practice.

With the aforementioned in mind, we present the following Deliberate Practice Plan Development and Implementation Rubric to help guide both your development as well as your implementation process (see Figure 11.1).

SUMMARY

This final chapter highlighted the importance of deep rather than superficial implementation of any initiative but, most importantly, the implementation of our Instructional Leadership Ability Framework. We made two recommendations for organizations to consider as antidotes to superficial implementation. The first recommendation was to create and use stories (case studies) of exemplary and proficient leadership practice around the leadership evaluation criteria to take highly effective leadership practice to scale. The second recommendation was for districts to generate and clearly define the words and phrases within the rubrics by providing word descriptions of expected leadership practice as a way to control for human variation within the system that naturally occurs when individuals are attempting to implement a new initiative.

Figure 11.1   Deliberate Practice Development and Implementation Rubric

Deliberate Practice (DP) Development Rubric

<u>Deliberate Practice Priorities</u>: The leader and the evaluator identify 1 to 2 specific and measurable priority learning goals related to teaching, learning, or school leadership practices that impact student learning growth. One or two targets are recommended.

Exemplary	Proficient	Progressing	Not Meeting Standard
All criteria for the proficient category have been successfully met. In addition: **The leader . . .** • Assists other leaders in helping them develop a proficient DP • Uses the concepts contained within the DP template to influence other school improvement planning documents • Frequently shares what he or she is learning (both successes and failures) about the effective development of DP plans with other schools, departments,	**The leader . . .** • Identifies a Prioritized Schoolwide Problem-of-Practice that clearly identifies the problem without offering any solutions. • Captures a SMART+ER Goal for his or her personal growth that aligns with a SMART+ER (e.g., specific, measurable, ambitious, relevant, time bound, evaluated, and re-evaluated) Goal within his or her School Improvement Plan • Identifies a few (1 or 2) sharply defined elements of their performance that offer the greatest opportunity to leverage his or her knowledge based on research, and skills (based on research) in multiple leadership performance areas that are designed to improve student achievement as **High-Impact Leadership Performance Areas** • Creates a single **Theory-of-Action** statement that specifically describes implicit or explicit models of how educators	**The leader . . .** • Identifies a **Prioritized School-wide Problem-of-Practice** that clearly identifies the problem but may offer solutions • Establishes a **SMART+ER Goal** that is either unrelated to one of the school's SMART Goals or attempts to focus on more than one SMART Goal within the school improvement plan • Identifies a few (1 or 2) **High-Impact Leadership Performance Areas;** however, the indicators selected may not be in areas that the research supports as high-effect size leadership practices • Represents the **Theory-of-Action** statement in the "IF/THEN" format, but the statement	**The leader . . .** • Is unable to produce a completed draft of his or her DP or several elements of the DP template are left blank • Selects a **Prioritized Goal** that is not connected to critica targets identified within the school improvement plan • Identifies more than three areas they believe are **High-Impact Leadership Performance Areas** and the indicators selected are not in areas the research supports as high-effect size leadership practices • Provides no **Theory-of-Action** statement, provides a statement that is not in an "IF/THEN" format, or fails

(Continued)

Figure 11.1 (Continued)

Deliberate Practice (DP) Development Rubric (Continued)

Exemplary	Proficient	Progressing	Not Meeting Standard
or districts to maximize the impact of the leader's personal learning experience	must act and what, as a result, he or she hypothesizes will happen to student achievement as a result aligned with the SMART+ER Goal • Constructs one to two **Leadership Strategy-in-Action** statements that are observable, subject to frequent public testing, and measurable (e.g., quantifiable; able to be gauged); these strategies are an obvious translation (i.e., paraphrased version) of the high-impact leadership practices and are constructed with formative language (e.g., increase the percentage of, etc.) and are time-bound (e.g., they indicate how often the public testing will occur)	lacks clarity or is overly complex and confusing and may not specifically address desired changes in student achievement related to the SMARTER+ER Goal • Designs the **Leadership Strategy-in-Action** statement but it does not clearly align with the Theory-of-Action statement. May not be stated in measurable terms, or it may resemble a task analysis • Creates the **Student Results** statement, which tends to be tied to assessments the school may or may not control and are measured less than on a monthly basis	to specifically identify the hypothesized adult practice and/or its desired impact on student achievement • Establishes little or no connection between the Theory-of-Action statement and the **Leadership Strategy-in-Action** statement • Creates the **Student Results** statement, which tends to be tied to large scale assessments rather than locally developed assessments that can be measured frequently • Identifies the **Qualitative Benefits** of the plan, which

Deliberate Practice (DP) Development Rubric (Continued)

Exemplary	Proficient	Progressing	Not Meeting Standard
	• Converts the results or "Then" statement from the Theory-of-Action into a measurable **Student Results** statement (a formative, teacher-made assessment related to the SMART+ER Goal) that is measured monthly • Identifies both the desired leadership and teacher benefits to conducting the research in the **Qualitative Benefits** column • Explains in clear terms the **Sources of Data** he or she intends to monitor (reflecting both the leadership as well as the student achievement data) • Provides a detailed **Task Analysis** that makes visible critical next steps.	• Identifies the **Qualitative Benefits**, which focuses primarily on how "others" will benefit but not on how the leader himself or herself will benefit from the successful improvement effort • Identifies the **Sources of Data to Monitor**, which tends to reflect the student achievement data but does not identify the data coming from the measurable Leadership Strategy-in-Action • Produces a **Task Analysis** but the list of things to do looks very similar to the items included within the Leadership-Strategy-in-Action step	tends to describe what the leader will do but does not describe the benefits the leader expects as a result of successfully implementing the Strategy-in-Action • Identifies the **Sources of Data to Monitor**, which tends to reflect the student achievement data but does not identify the data coming from the measurable Leadership Strategy-in-Action • Produces a **Task Analysis** but it includes non-key as well as key next steps and is too detailed to be of practical use

(Continued)

Figure 11.1 (Continued)

Deliberate Practice (DP) Implementation Rubric			
Exemplary	Proficient	Progressing	Not Meeting Standard
All criteria for the proficient category have been successfully met. In addition: **The leader . . .** • Shares the results of his or her action research with faculty, what he or she is learning, and how that learning will influence leadership practices in the future • Publicly reports, including plans and oral presentations, a frank acknowledgment of prior personal and organizational failures and provides clear suggestions for systemwide learning resulting from those lessons • Regularly shares the results of his or her action research along with some of the things they are learning about leadership practices and the connection to student achievement with other schools, departments, or districts to maximize the impact of the leader's personal learning experience	**The leader . . .** • Produces clear and consistent evidence that he or she is monitoring and measuring both the leadership strategy or strategies as well as the impact on student achievement monthly • Documents the changes in leadership practice that are occurring monthly as a result of the monitoring • Publicly displays the graphic depiction of the degree to which the achieved leadership strategies-in-action compare with the impact on student achievement	**The leader . . .** • Produces evidence that he or she is monitoring and measuring student effect data, but is inconsistent in monitoring and measuring leadership data. Consequently it is difficult to determine the degree to which the specified leadership practices are impacting student achievement • Participates in the action research process and provides limited evidence of changes based on data • May display student results data but has not yet created a graphic display depicting both the results of the leadership strategies-in-action compared with the changes in student performance	**The leader . . .** • Demonstrates no significant effort to work on the targets • Demonstrates an indifference to data, no changes in leadership practice compared to the previous year. The data screams "Change!" and the leader's actions say, "Everything is fine." • May not even be charting student results monthly let alone how educators are performing

Resources

The five elements of instructional leadership ability that are outlined in this book are aligned to the Interstate School Leadership Licensure Consortium (ISLLC) standards (see Figure R.1). The crosswalk in Figure R.1 should not imply that the authors believe that ISLLC is spot-on with their thinking; rather, this alignment provides a degree of confidence that the five elements are soundly established on contemporary policy regarding the knowledge and skills that principals must possess in order to be effective. Moreover, if we are operating from the same research base and conceptual framework, then it makes sense that the two sets of leadership expectations would align.

Professor Hattie (2009) mused that "feedback was most powerful when it is from the *student to the teacher*" (p. 173). A strategy to make certain that central office leaders are receiving and using the feedback from leaders to alter leadership practices that we have seen used is for

Figure R.1 Crosswalk of Instructional Leadership Ability Elements to ISLLC Standards

Instructional Leadership Ability Elements	Alignment With ISLLC Standards
Establishing a shared vision/mission, goals, and expectations	Standards 1, 2
Strategic resourcing	Standards 2, 3
Ensuring teacher and staff effectiveness	Standards 2, 3
Leading and participating in teacher/leader learning and development	Standards 1, 2, 3, 4, 5, 6
Providing an orderly, safe, and supportive environment	Standards 2, 3, 4, 5

supervisors to use a Feedback Response Sheet with school leaders (Figure R.2). The Feedback Response Sheet enables the supervisor to provide descriptive feedback to the school leader based on the success criteria (i.e., the descriptions of proficient leadership behavior) and then have the leader comment on how he or she intends to incorporate that feedback into future practice.

Figure R.2   Feedback Response Sheet

Task: _____		Grade Level Dept: _____
Name: _____		Date: _____
Look For	**Leader Feedback**	**Teacher Actions**
Below is a list of success criteria to use as you complete the activity	Compare this feedback with the Look For success criteria on the left	List specific ways you responded to leader feedback

Metacognition: Look at the feedback provided by the leader, and identify two specific steps to improve next time.

An example of a Shelby County POP plan that James Neihoff is currently using with his leadership team is depicted in Figure R.3.

The Nine Theories of Practice are described in Figure R.4.

Figure R.3 Sample of a Shelby County POP Plan

IMPLEMENTATION Component: "Blueprint" for Goal 1

Schoolwide Problem-of-Practice: Our MAP data show that our students are making growth in Reading but not the necessary growth required to bring students to the goal of every child experiencing at least one year's growth. Additionally, we are not ensuring that all students perform at or above grade level by the end of the year. This leads us to speculate that we are not guiding student learning expectations with learning targets that set the tone of the lesson, identify the trajectory of the lesson, and determine student success based on reflection of the lesson.

SMART Goal #1 Statement: A 29% increase of Kindergarten, 1st, 2nd, 3rd, 4th, and 5th-grade students will demonstrate a proficiency of 80% in English/ Language Arts by 05/31/2014 as measured by K-PREP for the 3rd, 4th, and 5th grades and by MAP and DRA for K, 1st, and 2nd grades.

Theories-of-Action: If we guide student learning expectations with learning targets that set the tone of the lesson, identify the trajectory of the lesson, and determine student success based on reflection of the lesson, then 80% of our students will be proficient in literacy according to MAP, KPREP, and DRA.

Construct Your Theories-in-Action (IF, THEN) Statements			
Leadership Implementation Strategies **IF** *I increase the percentage of (insert your 1–2 measurable leadership strategies)*	**Student Results Indicators** **THEN** *I expect to see an increase in the percentage of students "Proficient" or higher on...* *(Insert your student assessment)*	**Desired Benefits** *(Insert what you expect both you and students to achieve)*	**Sources of Data to Monitor** *(Insert what data you plan to monitor)*
1. If I provide monthly research-based (Learning Targets by Moss) professional learning opportunities for teachers 2. If I increase the amount of purposeful planning feedback utilizing anecdotal scripting coupled with conversations 3. If I increase classroom observations while utilizing the classroom observation tool	80% of our students will be proficient in literacy according to MAP, KPREP, and DRA.	1. Teachers will become so efficacious that no matter who is in their classroom, they know that the students will succeed. 2. Learning targets will become a vital part of the lesson that drives instruction. 3. An increase in student achievement as measured by common formative and summative assessments will take place. 4. All students will experience a year's worth of growth. 5. Students will perform at or above grade level.	1. Professional Learning Feedback Form 2. Observation feedback tool 3. Summative assessments

Figure R.4   Brief Description of the Nine Theories of Practice

Nine Theories of Practice	
Theory of Practice	**Brief Description(s)**
1. **Evaluating your impact**	Leaders believe that their most essential undertaking is to continuously seek feedback about their influences on students and, on the basis of the results, alter, enhance, or continue their teaching and/or leadership strategies.
2. **Activating change**	Leaders believe that success and failure in student learning are byproducts of their action or inaction. That is, they see themselves as agents of cognitive change, which requires a belief that student and/or adult achievement is not a fixed trait but rather is a dynamic, constantly changing characteristic as a result of teacher and leader dedication and hard work (Dweck, 2006).
3. **Focusing on learning more than teaching**	Leaders thrive on discussions about learning rather than on discussions about best practices in teaching and leadership.
4. **Viewing assessment as feedback about impact**	Leaders take the point of view that assessment (i.e., of leadership and/or teaching practice, student, teacher, parent/guardian perceptions) is feedback to them regarding their impact on student learning.
5. **Engaging in dialogue not monologue**	Leaders understand the power of engaging in active listening: listening to teachers, students, and parent/guardian perspectives.
6. **Embracing the challenge**	Leaders recognize that classroom as well as school life is a challenge for most students, teachers, and leaders and they need to accept, embrace, and shape the challenge into what they want it to be. In other words, the art of leading is that what is challenging to one teacher may not be to another.
7. **Developing relational trust**	Leaders highly regard their role in developing relational trust within classrooms and throughout the school. Why? Because there is persuasive evidence that links the level of trust among members of a school community and the way they work together and the level of social and academic progress of students.
8. **Teaching the academic vocabulary of learning**	Leaders recognize that the research overwhelmingly demonstrates that parent involvement in children's learning is positively related to increases in student achievement, which means leaders along with his or her staff must help parents understand the school's expectations along with the vocabulary used by teachers with their students to advance learning.
9. **Reinforcing that learning and leading is hard work**	Leaders know all too well and appreciate the fact that learning is not always enjoyable and easy. Often, learning is a messy, frustrating, nonlinear, recursive process that at times causes the learner to operate at a variety of levels of the knowledge continuum, co-constructing and re-constructing knowledge and ideas with others as they wrestle with challenging problems.

Bibliography

Astor, R. A., Benbenishty, R., & Estrada, J. N. (2009). School violence and theoretically atypical schools: The principal's centrality in orchestrating safe schools. *American Educational Research Journal, 46*(2), 423–461.

Barber, M., Moffit, A., & Kihn, P. (2011). *Deliverology 101: A field guide for educational leaders.* Thousand Oaks, CA: Corwin.

Black, P., Harrison, C., Lee, C., & William, D. (2003). *Assessment for learning: Putting it into practice.* New York, NY: Open University Press.

Boucher, M. M. (2013). *The relationship of principal conflict management style and school climate.* University of South Carolina, Educational Administration College of Education. Miriam Miley Boucher.

Bryan, W., & Harter, N. (1899). Studies on the telegraphic language: The acquisition of a hierarchy of habits. *Psychological Review, 6*, 345–375.

Bryk, A. S. (2010). Organizing schools for improvement. *Kappan, 91*(7), 23–30.

Bryk, A. S., & Schneider, B. L. (2002). *Trust in schools: A core resource for improvement.* New York: Russell Sage Foundation Publications.

Bryk, A. S., & Schneider, B. (2003). Trust in schools: A core resource for school reform. *Educational Leadership, 60*(6), 40–45.

Bryk, A. S., Sebring, P. B., Allensworth, E., Easton, J. Q., & Luppescu, S. (2010). *Organizing schools for improvement: Lessons from Chicago.* Chicago, IL: University of Chicago Press.

Canole, M., & Young, M. (2013). *Standards for educational leaders: An analysis.* Washington, DC: Council of Chief State School Officers.

Chappuis, J. (2005). Helping students understand assessment. *Educational Leadership, 63*(3), 39–43.

Clement, M. C. (2008, January/February). Improving teacher selection with behavior-based interviewing. *Principal,* 44–47.

Clifford, M., Menon, R., Gangi, T., Condon, C., & Hornung, K. (2012). *Measuring school climate for gauging principal performance.* Washington, DC: American Institutes for Research.

Clifford, M., & Ross, S. (2010). *Rethinking principal evaluation: A new paradigm informed by research and practice.* Alexandria, VA: National Association of Elementary School Principals.

Clifford, M., & Ross, S. (2011). *Designing principal evaluation systems: Research to guide decision-making.* Washington, DC: American Institutes for Research.

Collins, J. C., & Porras, J. I. (1994). *Built to last: Successful habits of visionary companies.* New York, NY: HarperBusiness.

Colvin, G. (2008). *Talent is overrated: What really separates world-class performers from everybody else.* New York: Penguin Group.

Connelly, S., Allen, M. T., & Waples, E. (2007). The impact of content and structure on a case-based approach to developing leadership skills. *International Journal Learning and Change, 2*(3), 218–249.

Covey, J. R. (1989). *The 7 habits of highly effective people: Powerful lessons in personal change.* New York, NY: Fireside.

Covey, S. R. (1994). *First things first.* New York, NY: Simon & Schuster.

Darling-Hammond, L., Wei, R. C., Andree, A., Richardson, N., & Orphanos, S. (2009). *Professional learning in the learning profession: A status report on teacher development in the United States.* Denver, CO: National Staff Development Council.

Davis, S., Kearney, K., Sanders, N., Thomas, C., & Leon, R. (2011). *The policies and practices of principal evaluation: A review of the literature.* San Francisco, CA: WestEd.

DiPaola, M. F., & Tschannen-Moran, M. (2005). Bridging or buffering? The impact of schools' adaptive strategies on student achievement. *Journal of Educational Administration, 43*(1), 60–71.

Durlak, J. A., Weissburg, R. P., Taylor, R. D., & Schellinger, K. B. (2011). The impact of enhancing students' social and emotional learning: A meta-analysis of school-based universal interventions. *Child Development, 82,* 405–432.

Dweck, C. S. (2006). *Mindset: The new psychology of success. How we can learn to fulfill our potential.* New York: Ballantine Books.

Epstein, J. L. (2010). *School, family, and community partnerships: Preparing educators and improving schools.* Boulder, CO: Westview Press.

Ericsson, K. (2000). *Expert performance and deliberate practice: An updated excerpt from Ericsson.* Retrieved June 19, 2013, from http://www.psy.fsu.edu/faculty/ericsson/ericsson.exp.perf.html

Fullan, M. (1998). *Change forces: Probing the depths of educational reform.* New York, NY: The Falmer Press.

Fullan, M. (2003). *The moral imperative of school leadership.* Thousand Oaks, CA: Corwin.

Fullan, M. (2008). *The six secrets of change: What the best leaders do to help their organizations survive and thrive.* San Francisco, CA: Jossey-Bass.

Fullan, M. (2010a). *All systems go: The change imperative for whole system reform.* Thousand Oaks, CA: Corwin.

Fullan, M. (2010b). *Motion leadership: The skinny on becoming change savvy.* Thousand Oaks, CA: Corwin.

Fullan, M., Hill, P., & Crevola, C. (2006). *Breakthrough.* Thousand Oaks, CA: Corwin.

Gallup Organization (n.d.). *Teacher insight assessment: Frequently asked questions.* Retrieved March 24, 2014, from http://www.gx.gallup.com/teacherinsight.gx

Gladwell, M. (2008). *Outliers: The story of success.* New York: Little, Brown and Company.

Goldring, E., Xiu, C. C., Murphy, J., Elliott, S. N., Carson, B., & Porter, A. C. (2008). "The evaluation of principals: What and how do states and districts assess leadership?" (presentation, Annual Meeting of American Educational Research Association, New York, NY, March 2008, pp. 1–40). Vanderbilt University.

Hall, G. E., & Hord, S. M. (2011). *Implementing change: Patterns, principles, and potholes* (3rd ed.). Boston, MA: Pearson.

Hattie, J. (2009). *Visible learning: A synthesis of over 800 meta-analyses relating to achievement.* New York, NY: Routledge.

Hattie, J. (2012a). *Visible learning for teachers: Maximizing impact on learning.* New York, NY: Routledge.

Hattie, J. (2012b). Know thy impact. *Educational Leadership, 70*(1), 18–23.

Hattie, J., & Timperley, H. (2007). The power of feedback. *Review of Educational Research, 77*(1), 81–112.

Hattie, J., & Yates, G. (2014). *Visible learning and the science of how we learn.* New York, NY: Rourtledge.

Henderson, A. T., & Mapp, K. L. (2002). *A new wave of evidence: The impact of school, family, and community connections on student achievement.* Austin, TX: Southwest Educational Department Laboratory.

Ingersoll, R. (2001). Teacher turnover and teacher shortages: An organizational analysis. *American Educational Research Journal, 38*(3), 499–534.

Jonsson, A., & Svingby, G. (2007). The use of scoring rubrics: Reliability, validity and educational consequences. *Educational Research Review, 2*, 130–144.

Kimball, S. M., Milanowski, A., & McKinney, S. A. (2009). Assessing the promise of standards-based performance evaluation for principals: Results from a randomized trial. *Leadership and Policy in Schools, 8*, 233–263.

Kluger, A., & DeNisi, A. (1996). The effects of feedback interventions on performance: A historical, review, a meta-analysis and a preliminary feedbak intervention theory. *Psychological Bulletin, 119*(2), 254–284.

Lacoe, J. R. (2011). *Too scared to learn? The academic consequences of feeling unsafe at school.* New York University, Graduate School of Public Service. New York, NY: New York University.

Latham, G. P., & Locke, E. A. (2006). Enhancing the benefits and overcoming the pitfalls of goal setting. *Organizational Dynamics, 35*(4), 332–340.

Leithwood, K. (2006). *Teacher working conditions that matter: Evidence for change.* Toronto, ON: Elementary Teachers' Federation of Ontario.

Leithwood, K., & Steinbach, R. (1995). *Expert problem solving: Evidence from school and district leaders.* Albany, NY: State University of New York Press.

Locke, E. A., & Latham, G. P. (2002). Building a practically useful theory of goal setting and task motivation: A 35-year odyssey. *American Psychologist, 57*(9), 705–717.

Louis, K. S., Leithwood, K., Wahlstrom, K. L., Anderson, S. A., Michlin, M., Mascall, B., et al. (2010). *Learning from leadership: Investigating the links to improved student learning.* St. Paul, MN: University of Minnesota.

Louis, M. R. (1980). Surprise and sense making: What newcomers experience in entering unfamiliar organizational settings. *Administrative Science Quarterly, 25*(2), 226–251.

Marzano, R. J., Kendall, J. S., & Gaddy, B. B. (1999). *Essential knowledge: The debate over what American students should know.* Aurora, CO: McREL Institute.

McRobbie, J. (2000). *Career-long teacher development: Policies that make sense.* Retrieved March 24, 2014, from WestEd Organization: www.wested.org/online/teacher_dev/TeacherDev.pdf

Miles, K. H., & Frank, S. (2008). *The strategic school: Making the most of people, time, and money.* Thousand Oaks, CA: Corwin.

Mitgang, L., Gill, J., & Cummins, H. J. (2013). *Districts matter: Cultivating the principals urban schools need.* New York, NY: The Wallace Foundation.

National Council for Accreditation of Teacher Education. (2010, November). *Transforming teacher education through clinical practice: A national strategy to prepare effective teachers.* Retrieved March 18, 2014, from www.ncate.org/publications: www.ncate.org/LinkClick.aspx?fileticket=zzeiB1OoqPK%3D&Tabid=715

National Research Council. (2000). *How people learn: Brain, mind, experience, and school.* Washington, DC.

Nelson, B., & Sassi, A. (2000). Shifting approaches to supervision: The case of mathematics supervision. *Educational Administration Quarterly, 36*(4), 553–584.

New Leaders for New Schools. (2010). *Evaluating principals: Balancing accountability with professional growth.* New York, NY: New Leaders for New Schools.

Newmann, F., Smith, B., Allensworth, E., & Bryk, A. (2001). Instructional program coherence: What it is and why it should guide school improvement policy. *Educational Evaluation and Policy Analysis, 23*(4), 297–321.

Nicol, D., & Macfarlane-Dick, D. (2006). Formative assessment and self-regulated learning: A model and seven principles of good feedback practice. *Studies in Higher Education, 3*(12), 199–218.

Popham, W. J. (2013). *Evaluating America's teachers: Mission possible?* Thousand Oaks, CA: Corwin.

Porter, A., Murphy, J., Goldring, E., Elliott, S. N., Polikoff, M. S., & May, H. (2008). *Vanderbilt assessment of leadership in education: Technical manual version 1.0.* Vanderbilt University.

Portin, B. S., Feldman, S., & Knapp, M. S. (2006). *Purposes, uses, and practices of leadership assessment in education.* Seattle: Center for the Study of Teaching and Policy, University of Washington.

Portin, B. S., Knapp, M. S., Dareff, S., Feldman, S., Russell, F. A., Samuelson, C., et al. (2009). *Leadership for learning improvement in urban schools.* Retrieved from Wallace Foundation Organization: http://www.wallacefoundation.org/knowledge-center/school-leadership/district-policy-and-practice/Pages/Leadership-for-Learning-Improvement-in-Urban-Schools.aspx

Reeves, D. B. (2009). *Assessing educational leaders: Evaluating performance for improved individual and organizational results* (2nd ed.). Thousand Oaks, CA: Corwin.

Reeves, D. B. (2011). *Finding your leadership focus: What matters most for student results.* New York, NY: Teachers College Press.

Robinson, V. (2011). *Student-centered leadership.* San Francisco, CA: Jossey-Bass.

Robinson, V., Hohepa, M., & Lloyd, C. (2009). *School leadership and student outcomes: Identifying what works and why.* University of Auckland. Wellington, NZ: New Zealand Ministry of Education.

Robinson, V. M. (2007). *School leadership and student outcomes: Identifying what works and why.* Winmalee, Australia: Australian Council for Educational Leaders.

Robinson, V. M. (2010). From instructional leadership to leadership capabilities: Empirical findings and methodological challenges. *Leadership and Policy in Schools, 9*, 1–26.

Robinson, V. M., Lloyd, C. A., & Rowe, K. J. (2008). The impact of leadership on student outcomes: An analysis of the differential effects of leadership types. *Educational Administration Quarterly, 44*(5), 645–674.

Sanders, N., Kearney, K., & Vince, S. (2012). *Using multiple forms of data in principal evaluations: An overview with examples.* San Francisco, CA: WestEd.

Sanders, W. L. (2000). Value-added assessment from student achievement data: Opportunities and hurdles. *Journal of Personnel Evaluation in Education, 14* (4), 329–339.

Saphier, J., Haley-Speca, M. A., & Gower, R. (2008). *The skillful teacher: Building your teaching skills.* Acton, MA: Research for Better Teaching, Inc.

Seashore-Louis, K., Leithwood, K., Wahlstrom, K. L., & Anderson, S. E. (2010). *Investigating the links to improved student achievement: Final report of research findings.* St. Paul, MN: University of Minnesota. Retrieved September 25, 2010, from http://www.cehd.umn.edu/carei/publications/documents/LearningFromLeadershipFinal.pdf.

Simon, H., & Chase, W.G. (1973). Skill in chess. *American Scientist, 61,* 394–403.

Smith, J. R. (2007). *Principal socialization: A phenomenological investigation.* School of Education. Denver, CO: Unpublished doctoral dissertation, University of Colorado at Denver Health Science Center.

Smith, R. L. (2007). *Organizational socialization: The lived experiences of four central office administrators.* School of Education. Denver, CO: Unpublished doctoral dissertation, University of Colorado at Denver Health Sciences Center.

Smith, R. L., Brofft, K., Law, N., & Smith, J. (2012). *The reflective leader: Implementing a multidimensional leadership performance system.* Englewood, CO: Lead + Learn Press.

Stiggins, R., Arter, J., Chappuis, J., & Chappuis, S. (2004). *Classroom assessment for student learning: Doing it right–using it well.* Princeton, NJ: National Testing Service.

Timperley, H., Wilson, A., Barrar, H., & Fung, I. (2007). *Teacher professional learning and development: Best evidence synthesis iteration [BES].* Wellington, NZ: Ministry of Education.

Toomer, T. (2013, September). *Broward assessment for school administrators: Deliberate practice growth target 2013–2014.* Ft. Lauderdale, FL: Broward County Public Schools.

U.S. Department of Education. (2012). *ESEA flexibility.* Washington, DC: Author.

Wahlstrom, K. L., Louis, K. S., Leithwood, K., & Anderson, S. A. (2010). *Investigating the links to improved student learning: Executive summary of research findings.* St. Paul, MN: Retrieved September 25, 2010, from http://www.cehd.umn.edu/carei/publications/documents/learning-from-leadership-exec-summary.pdf

Wiggins, G. (2012). Seven keys to effective feedback. *Educational Leadership, 70*(1), 11–16.

Wiliam, D. (2012). Feedback: Part of a system. *Educational Leadership, 70*(1), 30–34.

Yeh, S. S. (2006). *Raising student achievement through rapid assessment and test reform.* New York, NY: Teachers College Press.

Index

Academic vocabulary of learning (TOP 8):
  critical questions, 34*f*
  description, 32-34, 166*f*
Activating change (TOP 2):
  critical questions, 27*f*
  description, 25-26, 166*f*
Anderson, S. A., 131
Arizona Framework for Measuring
  Educator Effectiveness, 16
Assessing Educational Leaders (Reeves), 152
Assessment as feedback (TOP 4):
  critical questions, 28*f*
  description, 27-29, 166*f*
  rapid formative assessment, 28

Bees, Sherry, 120-121
Behavior-based interviewing (BBI), 58
Best Evidence Iteration Report (Robinson,
  Hohepa & Lloyd), 24

Canada, 94
Capability:
  relational trust development, 32
  theories of practice, 23, 24, 32
Cognition Education (New Zealand),
  48-49, 129
Colorado Principal Evaluation
  Framework, 16, 17
Common Core State Standards
  (CCSS), 47-48, 134
Communication skills, 9*f*, 11-12
Concord Junior High School (Elkhart,
  Indiana), 143-144, 145*f*

Data-sources-to-monitor statement,
  138, 139*f*
Deliberate Practice Development Rubric:
  exemplary leadership, 159-162*f*

not-meeting-expectations leadership,
  159-162*f*
proficient leadership, 159-162*f*
progressing leadership, 159-162*f*
Deliberate Practice Plan (DPP):
  components of, 126-141
  data-sources-to-monitor statement,
    138, 139*f*
  defined, 124-126
  high-impact leadership practices,
    130-133
  principal-evaluation systems, 124
  problem-of-practice statement,
    126-128, 129*f*
  qualitative benefits statement, 137, 138*f*
  sample data-sources-to-monitor
    statement, 139*f*
  sample high-impact leadership
    practices, 132*f*
  sample plan, 140-141*f*
  sample problem-of-practice
    statement, 129*f*
  sample qualitative benefits
    statement, 138*f*
  sample SMART+ER Goal
    statement, 130*f*
  sample strategy-in-action
    statement, 136*f*
  sample student results statement, 137*f*
  sample task analysis statement, 140*f*
  sample theory-of-action statement, 135*f*
  SMART+ER Goal statement, 128-130
  strategy-in-action statement, 134-136
  student results statement, 137
  summary, 142
  task analysis statement, 138-141
  template for, 125f, 127*f*
  theory-of-action statement, 133-134, 135*f*

Deliberate Practice Plan (DPP) application:
  Concord Junior High School (Elkhart, Indiana), 143-144, 145*f*
  graphing data, 144, 146, 147-148, 149-150
  Lyons Creek Middle School (Fort Lauderdale, Florida), 148-150
  Shelby County School District (Kentucky), 146-148
  summary, 150

Embracing the challenge (TOP 6):
  critical questions, 31*f*
  description, 29-30, 166*f*
Engaging in dialogue (TOP 5):
  critical questions, 30*f*
  description, 29, 166*f*
  teacher voice, 29
Environmental support:
  clear expectations, 92-93
  conflict resolution, 94-95
  description, 10f, 38, 92-95, 98-99*f*
  evidence of impact, 96
  examples, 101-102*f*
  exemplary leadership, 98-102*f*
  instructional disruptions, 93-94
  ISLLC Standards alignment, 163*f*
  leadership attributes, 99-100*f*
  not-meeting-expectations leadership, 98-102*f*
  proficient leadership, 98-102*f*
  progressing leadership, 98-102*f*
  rationale for, 92
  rubric for, 97, 98-102*f*
  summary, 96-97
Ethics, 9f, 11, 13
Evaluating America's Teachers (Popham), 5
Evaluating impact (TOP 1):
  critical questions, 26*f*
  description, 24-25, 166*f*
Exemplary leadership:
  Deliberate Practice Development Rubric, 159-162*f*
  description, 38f, 39-40
  environmental support, 98-102*f*
  examples, 39*f*
  shared vision/goal setting, 51-54*f*
  strategic resourcing, 62-66*f*
  teacher/leader development, 85-89*f*
  teacher/staff effectiveness, 72-77*f*

Feedback for learning:
  cultural environment for, 115-116
  defined, 104-105

effectiveness criteria, 108-111, 116, 117-118, 121
examples, 106-108, 109-111, 118-121
feedback levels, 111-115
Feedback Response Sheet, 117, 164*f*
importance of, 103-104
principal-evaluation framework, 106, 118-120
principal-evaluation systems, 105-106
process feedback, 111, 112, 113*f*
ratiocination process, 121
research literature on, 104-106
self feedback, 111, 114-115
self-regulation feedback, 111, 112-114
self-regulation skills, 116-117
summary, 122
sustainable feedback, 120-121
task feedback, 111-112
Fixed mindset, 23
Florida Personnel Evaluation System, 16
Focusing on learning (TOP 3):
  critical questions, 28*f*
  description, 26-27, 166*f*

Gator Run Elementary School (Fort Lauderdale, Florida), 109-111
Gladwell, M., 123
Google Bump, The, 146
Growth mindset, 23

Harris, Tucker, 119-120
Hattie, J., 7, 10, 23, 26, 105, 129
High-impact leadership practices, 130-133
Hohepa, M., 24
How People Learn (National Research Council), 104

Instructional leadership ability elements:
  leadership ability framework, 22f, 35-38
  principal-evaluation framework, 9f, 10f, 11
  See also Environmental support; Shared vision/goal setting; Strategic resourcing; Teacher/leader development; Teacher/staff effectiveness
Instructional leadership ability framework:
  elements of, 22f, 35-38
  leadership performance levels, 38-43
  model illustration, 22*f*
  Theories of Practice (TOP), 22f, 23-35
Instructional Leadership Ability Rubric:
  environmental support, 97, 98-102*f*

shared vision/goal setting, 50, 51-54*f*
strategic resourcing, 61, 62-66*f*
teacher/leader development, 84, 85-89*f*
teacher/staff effectiveness, 71, 72-77*f*
Instructional leadership ability training:
case study approach, 152-155
guidelines for, 151
rubric approach, 155-158, 159-162*f*
Instructional resources, 60
Integrity, 32
Interstate School Leaders Licensure
Consortium (ISLLC) Standards, 3, 4,
5-6, 7*f*, 163*f*
*Investigating the Links to Improved
Student Learning* (Wahlstrom, Louis,
Leithwood, & Anderson), 131
Israel, 92-93

Leadership performance levels:
exemplary leadership, 38f, 39-40
not-meeting-expectations leadership,
38f, 42-43
proficient leadership, 38f, 40-41
progressing leadership, 38f, 41, 42*f*
summary, 38*f*
See also specific level
Learning is hard work (TOP 9):
critical questions, 35*f*
description, 34-35, 166*f*
Leithwood, K., 131
Linking-talk dialogue, 69
Lloyd, C., 24
Louis, K. S., 131
Lyons Creek Middle School (Fort
Lauderdale, Florida), 148-150

Maplewood Elementary School (Fort
Lauderdale, Florida), 120-121
Maryland Educator Evaluation System, 16
Mid-continent Regional Educational
Laboratory (McREL), 5-6, 8-9*f*
Mindframe, 23, 24
Mindset, 23, 24

National Association of Elementary
School Principals, 14-15
National Association of Secondary
School Principals, 14-15
National Board Standards for
Accomplished Principals, 5-6, 7*f*
National Research Council, 104
Neihof, James, 106-108, 146-148
New Leaders for New Schools, 15, 18-19

New Leaders Principal Evaluation
System, 16
New York City, 93
New York City Principal Performance
Review, 16
Not-meeting-expectations leadership:
Deliberate Practice Development
Rubric, 159-162*f*
description, 38f, 42-43
environmental support, 98-102*f*
examples, 42*f*
shared vision/goal setting, 51-54*f*
strategic resourcing, 62-66*f*
teacher/leader development, 85-89*f*
teacher/staff effectiveness, 72-77*f*

Outliers (Gladwell), 123

Peters, Keith, 109-111
Pine Trail Elementary School (Florida),
119-120
Plan on a Page (POP), 107, 165*f*
Popham, W. J., 5
Power of Feedback, The (Hattie &
Timperley), 105
Principal Evaluation Committee
(2010), 14-15
Principal-evaluation framework:
communication skills, 9f, 11-12
ethics, 9f, 11, 13
evaluative criteria selection, 5-13
evaluative weight adjustment, 6f, 17-19
evaluative weight designation,
6f, 16-17, 18*f*
evidence source identification, 6f, 14-16
feedback for learning, 106, 118-120
instructional leadership ability
elements, 9f, 10f, 11
leadership assessment, 16, 17, 20*f*
model illustration, 6*f*
national leadership standards, 5-6, 7f,
8-9*f*
professional growth, 16, 17, 20*f*
ratings of leader performance, 16, 17, 20*f*
rubric development, 6f, 13, 14*f*
sample rubric template, 14*f*
student learning, 16, 17, 20*f*
summative evaluation, 6f, 19, 20*f*
teacher effectiveness, 16, 17, 20*f*
transformational leadership, 11
Principal-evaluation systems:
Deliberate Practice Plan (DPP), 124
feedback for learning, 105-106

improvement efforts, 3-4
limitations of, 1-3
Principal Professional Growth and
    Effectivenss System (PPGES), 107
Problem-of-practice statement,
    126-128, 129f
Process feedback, 111, 112, 113f
Proficient leadership:
    Deliberate Practice Development
        Rubric, 159-162f
    description, 38f, 40-41
    environmental support, 98-102f
    examples, 40f
    shared vision/goal setting, 51-54f
    strategic resourcing, 62-66f
    teacher/leader development, 85-89f
    teacher/staff effectiveness, 72-77f
Progressing leadership:
    Deliberate Practice Development
        Rubric, 159-162f
    description, 38f, 41
    environmental support, 98-102f
    examples, 42f
    shared vision/goal setting, 51-54f
    strategic resourcing, 62-66f
    teacher/leader development, 85-89f
    teacher/staff effectiveness, 72-77f

Qualitative benefits statement, 137, 138f

Rapid formative assessment, 28
Ratiocination process, 121
Reeves, D., 152
Relational trust development (TOP 7):
    capability, 32
    critical questions, 33f
    description, 31-32, 166f
    integrity, 32
    respect, 31
    wisdom, 31-32
Respect, 31
Robinson, V. M., 24

Self feedback, 111, 114-115
Self-regulation feedback, 111, 112-114
Shared vision/goal setting:
    description, 10f, 36, 46-49, 51-52f
    evidence of impact, 49-50
    examples, 53-54f
    exemplary leadership, 51-54f
    ISLLC Standards alignment, 163f
    leadership attributes, 10f, 36, 46-49,
        51-552-53f2f

not-meeting-expectations leadership,
    51-54f
proficient leadership, 51-54f
progressing leadership, 51-54f
rationale for, 45-46
rubric for, 50, 51-54f
SMART+ER Goal, 48-49
SMART Goal, 48
standards-based instruction, 47-48
summary, 50
Shelby County School District (Kentucky):
    Deliberate Practice Plan (DPP), 146-148
    feedback for learning, 106-108
    Plan on a Page (POP), 107, 165f
    Principal Professional Growth and
        Effectivenss System (PPGES), 107
SMART+ER Goal:
    Deliberate Practice Plan (DPP), 128-130
    shared vision/goal setting, 48-49
SMART Goal, 48, 129
South Carolina, 95
Staff resources, 56-59
Standards-based instruction:
    ISLLC Standards, 3, 4, 5-6, 7f, 163f
    shared vision/goal setting, 47-48
    theory-of-action statement, 134
Strategic resourcing:
    behavior-based interviewing (BBI), 58
    description, 10f, 36-37, 56-60, 62-63f
    evidence of impact, 60-61
    examples, 65-66f
    exemplary leadership, 62-66f
    instructional resources, 60
    instructional time, 59-60
    ISLLC Standards alignment, 163f
    leadership attributes, 63-64f
    not-meeting-expectations leadership,
        62-66f
    proficient leadership, 62-66f
    progressing leadership, 62-66f
    rationale for, 55-56
    rubric for, 61, 62-66f
    staff, 56-59
    summary, 61
    teacher recruitment, 57-58
    teacher retention, 58-59
Strategy-in-action statement, 134-136
Student results statement, 137

Task analysis statement, 138-141
Task feedback, 111-112
TeacherInsight, 57-58
Teacher/leader development:

case study approach, 152-154
description, 10f, 37, 81-82, 85-86f
evidence of impact, 80-81, 82-83
examples, 88-89f
exemplary leadership, 85-89f
ISLLC Standards alignment, 163f
leadership attributes, 86-88f
not-meeting-expectations leadership,
    85-89f
proficient leadership, 85-89f
progressing leadership, 85-89f
rationale for, 80-81
rubric for, 84, 85-89f
summary, 83-84
Teacher recruitment, 57-58
Teacher retention, 58-59
Teacher/staff effectiveness:
    description, 10f, 37, 68-70, 72-73f
    evidence of impact, 70-71
    examples, 76-77f
    exemplary leadership, 72-77f
    ISLLC Standards alignment, 163f
    leadership attributes, 74-75f
    linking-talk dialogue, 69
    not-meeting-expectations leadership,
        72-77f
    proficient leadership, 72-77f
    progressing leadership, 72-77f
    rationale for, 68
    rubric for, 71, 72-77f
    summary, 71
Teacher voice, 29
Tennessee Teacher and Principal
    Evaluation Policy, 16
Theories of Practice (TOP):
    academic vocabulary of learning (TOP 8),
        32-34, 166f
    activating change (TOP 2), 25-26, 27f, 166f
    assessment as feedback (TOP 4),
        27-29, 166f

capabilities, 23, 24
description, 166f
embracing the challenge (TOP 6),
    29-30, 31f, 166f
engaging in dialogue (TOP 5), 29,
    30f, 166f
evaluating impact (TOP 1), 24-25,
    26f, 166f
focusing on learning (TOP 3), 26-27,
    28f, 166f
learning is hard work (TOP 9), 34-35,
    166f
mindframe, 23, 24
mindset, 23, 24
model illustration, 22f
relational trust development (TOP 7),
    31-32, 33f, 166f
Theory-of-action statement:
    Deliberate Practice Plan (DPP),
        133-134, 135f
    enacted theories, 134
    intended theories, 134
Time resources, 59-60
Timperley, H., 105
Toomer, Ted, 148-150

Using Multiple Forms of Data in Principal
    Evaluations (WestEd), 15-16

Vanderbilt Assessment of Leadership in
    Education (VAL-ED), 5-6, 8-9f, 15
Visible Learning (Hattie), 7, 10, 23, 26, 129

Wahlstrom, K. L., 131
Washington D.C. Public Schools
    Effectiveness Assessment System for
    School-Based Personnel: IMPACT, 16
Wisdom, 31-32

Zook, Rob, 143-144, 145f

A SAGE Company

Corwin is committed to improving education for all learners by publishing books and other professional development resources for those serving the field of PreK–12 education. By providing practical, hands-on materials, Corwin continues to carry out the promise of its motto: **"Helping Educators Do Their Work Better."**